Scars Unseen

Charles Wilson

Published by Revvity, Inc, 2025.

SCARS UNSEEN

First edition. August 27, 2025.

Written by Charles Wilson.

Table of Contents

INTRODUCTION: THE INVISIBLE WOUNDS

The Unseen Battlefields

When we think of wounds, most of us imagine the visible ones scars across the skin, broken bones in a cast, or surgical stitches pulling tissue back together. These are injuries we can recognize and point to, injuries that earn sympathy and validation. But there exists another kind of wound, one that leaves no obvious trace on the surface yet lingers with devastating force. These are the wounds of trauma: invisible injuries that live in the mind, body, and spirit long after the danger has passed.

For centuries, societies struggled to name and understand these hidden scars. Soldiers returned from wars with trembling hands, haunted eyes, and sudden fits of rage or despair. Survivors of accidents and disasters found themselves trapped in loops of relived terror. Children who endured abuse grew into adults who could not easily love, trust, or feel at home in their own skin. Yet for much of history, these experiences were dismissed as weakness, madness, or moral failing. Only in recent decades have we begun to recognize trauma for what it truly is: a fundamental reshaping of the brain and body's survival systems, a condition as real and as deserving of care as any physical disease.

This book is about that recognition how we came to see trauma, how we learned to trace its pathways through the nervous system, and how we are beginning to discover ways of healing that go beyond words alone. It is also about the people who carried the burden of trauma before the science had a name for it, and the pioneers who listened to their stories closely enough to reshape medicine itself.

Why Trauma Matters Now

We live in a world where trauma is both more visible and more hidden than ever. On the one hand, headlines constantly remind us of wars, refugee crises, mass shootings, natural disasters, and epidemics of domestic violence and child abuse. The language of "trauma" has entered mainstream conversations, used in classrooms, workplaces, and public debates. Yet at the same time, many who suffer its effects do so in silence. They may not even recognize their struggles as trauma, or they may fear the stigma of appearing broken or weak.

The importance of understanding trauma extends far beyond the individuals who carry it. Trauma ripples outward, shaping families, communities, and entire societies. Children raised in violent homes carry altered stress systems into adulthood, influencing their health, relationships, and even the next generation. Veterans returning from war affect not only themselves but also their spouses, children, and communities. When we ignore trauma, we pay the price in public health crises rising addiction rates, cycles of violence, chronic illness, and mental health epidemics.

To understand trauma is to understand a hidden architecture beneath much of human suffering. And to face it honestly is to open the door to a more compassionate, resilient future.

A Brief History of Silence

Although trauma may feel like a modern discovery, its footprints stretch far back into history. Ancient Greek historians wrote of soldiers overcome by "battle madness." In Shakespeare's plays, war veterans appear restless, sleepless, and prone to sudden rages. During the American Civil War, doctors spoke of "irritable heart" and "soldier's heart" when confronted with men who suffered palpitations, breathlessness, and exhaustion long after combat.

In World War I, thousands of soldiers developed what came to be known as "shell shock" a condition marked by trembling, nightmares, and paralysis without visible injury. At first, it was believed to result from physical damage caused by exploding shells. When doctors realized that soldiers who had never been near blasts displayed the same symptoms, the unsettling truth emerged: the mind itself could break under overwhelming stress.

Yet even then, trauma was not fully legitimized. Some soldiers were treated with sympathy and rest, while others were branded as cowards or deserters. Military systems often saw psychological collapse as a moral weakness rather than a medical condition. The stigma lingered through World War II, where traumatized soldiers were diagnosed with "combat fatigue" but encouraged or forced to return to battle.

It was not until the Vietnam War that the silence began to truly fracture. Veterans returned home with deep psychological wounds, and unlike earlier wars, they faced not parades and public support but social hostility. Many turned to drugs, alcohol, or isolation to numb their pain. Suicide rates soared. The medical system struggled to categorize what was happening was it depression, psychosis, or something new? Out of their suffering, and through the persistence of both survivors and clinicians, the modern diagnosis of **Post-Traumatic Stress Disorder (PTSD)** was born in 1980.

The Rediscovery of Trauma

The naming of PTSD was more than a medical milestone; it was a revolution in listening. For the first time, the psychiatric establishment recognized that extreme experiences combat, rape, disasters could leave long-lasting psychological imprints even in people who had previously been healthy and resilient.

This recognition, however, was not granted easily. It came through testimony veterans speaking out about their nightmares, flashbacks, and rage; women demanding acknowledgment of the psychological cost of sexual assault and domestic violence; therapists who refused to reduce their patients' suffering to abstract diagnostic labels. Trauma was rediscovered because survivors insisted their pain was real, even when society wanted to turn away.

The Science of Survival

The emergence of PTSD opened the door to scientific inquiry. What exactly happens in the brain during trauma? Why do survivors experience flashbacks that feel more like reliving than remembering? Why does the body continue to react to danger long after safety has been restored?

Early neuroscience began to show that trauma was not just a psychological wound but a biological one. Brain imaging revealed that trauma altered the balance between the **amygdala** (the brain's alarm system), the **hippocampus** (the memory processor), and the **prefrontal cortex** (the center of reasoning and regulation). Stress hormones like cortisol and adrenaline flooded the body, reshaping circuits of fear and survival. In essence, trauma reprograms the body to remain on high alert, even when the threat is gone.

This insight changed everything. Trauma was no longer seen solely as a narrative of the past but as a present-tense condition imprinted in the nervous system. It explained why survivors could not simply "move on" or "forget." Their bodies carried the memory in every cell.

Trauma as a Universal Human Experience

One of the most important truths about trauma is that it is not rare. While not everyone experiences war, disaster, or abuse, almost everyone will face moments that overwhelm their capacity to cope. Some may recover naturally, while others are left with lasting imprints that shape the course of their lives. Trauma, in this sense, is part of the human condition.

By understanding trauma, we learn something about the human capacity for both vulnerability and resilience. We see how survival mechanisms that once saved our ancestors hyperalertness to danger, bodily freeze responses, deep memory imprints of fear can become maladaptive in modern contexts. We also see how healing often requires us to return to the most basic elements of humanity: safety, connection, storytelling, and embodiment.

From Silence to Voice

The story of trauma is also a story of silence and voice. For centuries, survivors' voices were dismissed, pathologized, or ignored. The hysterical women of the nineteenth century, the "shell-shocked" soldiers of World War I, the "weak" or "unstable" veterans of Vietnam all were burdened not only with their suffering but with society's refusal to believe them. Only when enough voices spoke together did psychiatry begin to listen.

This shift did not happen in laboratories alone. It happened in the testimony of veterans who demanded recognition, in the advocacy of women who insisted their abuse mattered, in the persistence of clinicians who sat with their patients long enough to see patterns others dismissed. Trauma was rediscovered not by discovering something new in nature, but by finally listening to what had always been there.

The Social Costs of Unhealed Trauma

Unhealed trauma does not stay confined within individuals. It spills into families, neighborhoods, and generations. Children raised by traumatized parents often inherit patterns of fear and instability, even if they never experience abuse themselves. Communities ravaged by war, colonization, or systemic violence carry collective scars that persist for decades. Entire nations can be shaped by unacknowledged wounds, perpetuating cycles of conflict and mistrust.

Public health research now confirms what survivors have long known: trauma is a root cause of many of society's greatest challenges. The landmark **Adverse Childhood Experiences (ACE) study** demonstrated that children exposed to abuse, neglect, or household dysfunction face dramatically higher risks of addiction, depression, heart disease, and early death. Trauma is not a private misfortune it is a public health emergency.

Hope in Healing

Although trauma can leave deep imprints, this book is also about hope. Neuroscience shows that the brain is plastic it can change and rewire throughout life. Communities show that safety and connection can restore what isolation and violence once broke. Therapies that involve the body, creativity, and presence demonstrate that healing does not have to be confined to words alone.

If trauma reshapes the brain, so can recovery. If trauma isolates, healing can reconnect. If trauma silences, healing can give voice.

This book begins, then, not only with the story of trauma's wounds but with the possibility of transformation. By the end, the hope is not merely to understand trauma, but to see new paths forward for survivors, for caregivers, and for society at large.

and respond flexibly to challenges. In trauma survivors, however, this system is disrupted.

- **Triggers** activate the amygdala before the prefrontal cortex has time to assess the situation. The body reacts to danger that isn't there.
- **Hypervigilance** keeps survivors constantly scanning their environment, unable to fully relax or trust.
- **Emotional reactivity** swings between extremes: rage, panic, shutdown. Survivors may feel controlled by their reactions rather than in control of them.

Over time, this hijacking erodes a person's sense of agency. Instead of feeling like the pilot of their own life, they feel like a passenger being yanked around by invisible forces. The self becomes fractured, not because of weakness, but because trauma has rewired the brain's survival circuits.

The Unspoken Legacy of Trauma

As devastating as flashbacks and hypervigilance can be, perhaps the most corrosive legacy of trauma is **shame.** Survivors often blame themselves for what happened, even when the fault clearly lies elsewhere. A child may believe they caused their own abuse; a soldier may feel guilty for surviving when comrades did not; a rape survivor may carry the weight of silence imposed by disbelief or blame.

This shame breeds **secrecy**. Survivors may feel that their pain is unspeakable, that no one could understand, or that revealing it would lead to rejection. Silence becomes a second wound layered on top of the first.

Shame and silence isolate survivors from the very connections that could help them heal. Unable to share their truth, they withdraw. Friends and loved ones may sense the distance but not understand its cause. Over time, isolation deepens, reinforcing the false belief that trauma has set them apart from the rest of humanity.

Trauma as Isolation

At its core, trauma is not just the experience of terror it is the experience of being **alone in terror**. Whether in war, abuse, or disaster, the common thread is that survivors faced the unbearable without the presence of safety, support, or protection. This is what sears the trauma so deeply into memory: the sense of isolation.

The aftermath often repeats the pattern. Survivors withdraw because they feel misunderstood; others withdraw because they feel helpless to help. The cycle of trauma thus perpetuates isolation.

Yet it is precisely in connection that healing begins. Neuroscience confirms that the nervous system is not self-contained it is regulated through relationships. A child calms when held by a caregiver; an adult survivor calms when seen, heard, and believed by another. Trauma isolates, but recovery reconnects.

The Imprint Beyond the Individual

Trauma does not stop at the boundary of the individual. Its imprints ripple outward into families and communities. Parents carrying unresolved trauma may inadvertently transmit patterns of hypervigilance or emotional shutdown to their children. Communities scarred by violence may carry collective memories of fear, mistrust, and grief.

Shame and silence perpetuate cycles. What is unspoken in one generation is often reenacted in the next. Breaking the cycle requires more than individual therapy it requires cultural spaces where trauma can be named, witnessed, and transformed.

Toward Healing the Imprint

Understanding the imprint of trauma is not an end in itself but a beginning. By recognizing that trauma is not weakness but biology, not personal failing but survival, we begin to replace shame with compassion. By naming the ways trauma hijacks the brain, we give survivors a language for what once felt unspeakable. By breaking the silence, we open the door to connection.

The imprint of trauma may be lasting, but it is not unchangeable. Just as the nervous system was shaped by terror, it can be reshaped by safety. Just as isolation deepened the wound, connection can begin to heal it.

The next section will turn toward that healing examining the limits of traditional talk therapy, the rise of innovative approaches like EMDR and neurofeedback, and the powerful role of community, creativity, and the body in recovery.

CHAPTER ONE: LESSONS FROM VIETNAM VETERANS

Introduction

The modern recognition of trauma as a legitimate psychiatric and medical phenomenon owes much to the experiences of soldiers returning from the Vietnam War. While trauma had been observed in earlier conflicts described variously as "shell shock" in World War I and "combat fatigue" in World War II it was Vietnam that forced psychiatry, and indeed society, to confront the long-term psychological effects of war in a sustained and systematic way.

Vietnam veterans became the unwitting pioneers of a new era of trauma studies. Their struggles to reintegrate into civilian life, to manage symptoms that had no name, and to seek acknowledgment from institutions that often dismissed or pathologized them, laid the foundation for the diagnosis of post-traumatic stress disorder (PTSD). This chapter examines their experiences, the societal reactions they provoked, and the profound lessons that emerged from their suffering.

The Context of the Vietnam War

The Vietnam War differed from previous American conflicts in several respects, all of which shaped the psychological aftermath for returning soldiers.

- **The Nature of Combat**: Unlike the large-scale battles of World War II, Vietnam was marked by guerrilla warfare, ambushes, and an enemy that was often indistinguishable from civilians. This produced a chronic sense of uncertainty and vigilance; danger could emerge from any direction, at any moment.
- **The Length of Deployment**: Soldiers typically served one-year tours, after which they were rotated out individually rather than returning home as cohesive units. This practice deprived many of the communal support that had previously been critical for processing the experience of war.
- **The Moral Ambiguity**: Vietnam was not framed as a clear moral struggle, as World War II had been. Questions about the legitimacy of

U.S. involvement, combined with highly publicized atrocities such as the My Lai massacre, left many soldiers with profound moral injuries feelings of guilt, shame, and betrayal that exceeded the traditional scope of combat stress.

- **The Reception at Home**: Perhaps most significantly, veterans returned to a society divided and often hostile. Unlike the celebrations that greeted World War II veterans, many Vietnam veterans were met with indifference or even contempt. This lack of validation compounded their isolation and exacerbated psychological wounds.

These unique features of Vietnam created conditions under which trauma would not only manifest acutely but also persist chronically, reshaping lives for decades.

Symptoms Without a Name

Upon returning home, countless veterans experienced symptoms that today would be recognized as classic PTSD:

- **Flashbacks and Nightmares**: Veterans reported intrusive recollections of combat, often triggered by loud noises, crowded spaces, or even the smell of smoke. Nightmares disrupted sleep, leaving them exhausted and irritable.
- **Hypervigilance**: Many described feeling perpetually on guard, scanning their environments for threats even in mundane settings such as grocery stores or family gatherings.
- **Emotional Numbing**: Some found themselves unable to connect with loved ones, describing themselves as "hollow" or "cut off." Joy, intimacy, and trust seemed inaccessible.
- **Explosive Anger**: Irritability and sudden outbursts strained marriages, friendships, and employment.
- **Substance Abuse**: Drugs and alcohol became common coping mechanisms, offering temporary relief from intrusive symptoms but creating cycles of dependence.

At the time, however, these experiences were not well understood. Psychiatry lacked a diagnostic framework for chronic trauma responses. The existing model of "combat fatigue" assumed symptoms would resolve once soldiers were removed from the battlefield. When symptoms persisted, veterans were often misdiagnosed with personality disorders, depression, or substance dependence, rather than recognized as suffering from a coherent trauma syndrome.

The Struggle for Recognition

Veterans' advocacy played a crucial role in the eventual recognition of PTSD. By the early 1970s, growing numbers of veterans began to organize, forming groups such as the Vietnam Veterans Against the War (VVAW). While initially political, these groups soon became sites of mutual support, where veterans shared experiences of psychological suffering.

This collective storytelling challenged the dominant narrative that only the weak or maladjusted struggled after war. Veterans argued that their symptoms were not personal failings but direct consequences of exposure to overwhelming combat stress. The act of bearing witness to each other and to the public was itself a form of healing, but it was also a demand for institutional acknowledgment.

Psychologists and psychiatrists who worked closely with these veterans, particularly in community-based "rap groups," began to document consistent patterns across cases. These grassroots observations eventually pressured the psychiatric establishment to reconsider its framework. When the **Diagnostic and Statistical Manual of Mental Disorders (DSM-III)** was published in 1980, PTSD was included as a new diagnostic category a direct legacy of Vietnam veterans' advocacy and suffering.

Lessons in the Nature of Trauma

The experiences of Vietnam veterans offered several critical lessons that transformed the understanding of trauma:

1. **Trauma is Persistent**: Unlike earlier assumptions that combat stress would dissipate with time, veterans demonstrated that trauma could endure for decades, shaping entire lifespans if untreated.
2. **Trauma is Multifaceted**: Veterans showed that trauma is not limited to intrusive memories but includes physiological hyperarousal,

emotional withdrawal, moral injury, and interpersonal dysfunction.

3. **Trauma Requires Validation**: The lack of societal recognition exacerbated veterans' suffering. Stigma and dismissal often worsened symptoms, while validation and support were protective.
4. **Trauma is Political**: The war's controversy meant that veterans' trauma could not be separated from the broader political context. Their suffering was entangled with national debates about morality, justice, and accountability.

The Legacy of Vietnam Veterans

The legacy of Vietnam veterans extends beyond the diagnostic recognition of PTSD. Their struggles reshaped clinical practice, public discourse, and cultural representations of trauma.

- **Clinical Practice**: Therapies began to shift toward acknowledging and processing traumatic memories, rather than dismissing them or attributing them to character flaws.
- **Public Awareness**: Films, literature, and media began to depict the psychological scars of war, influencing how subsequent generations understood the costs of conflict.
- **Policy and Research**: Federal funding for veteran mental health services increased, and research into trauma expanded dramatically, laying the groundwork for the neuroscience revolution described in later chapters.

Perhaps most importantly, the lessons of Vietnam extended beyond combat. As psychiatrists and psychologists began to recognize the universality of trauma responses, the framework developed for veterans was soon applied to survivors of rape, domestic violence, childhood abuse, and natural disasters. Vietnam veterans thus opened the door for a much broader societal acknowledgment of trauma.

Conclusion

The experiences of Vietnam veterans represent a pivotal moment in the history of trauma studies. Their suffering challenged assumptions about resilience, forced psychiatry to expand its diagnostic categories, and highlighted the essential role of validation and community in recovery. They taught us that trauma is not merely an acute reaction to danger but a chronic condition that reshapes memory, perception, and identity.

The lessons learned from Vietnam set the stage for a revolution in understanding trauma one that would eventually encompass neuroscience, developmental psychology, and somatic therapies. Above all, they underscored a truth that continues to guide the field: trauma cannot be healed in silence. Recognition, community, and compassionate engagement are essential steps on the path to recovery.

CHAPTER TWO: ORIGINS OF PTSD DIAGNOSIS

Introduction

The recognition of **post-traumatic stress disorder (PTSD)** as an official psychiatric diagnosis in 1980 marked a watershed moment in the history of mental health. For the first time, the enduring psychological consequences of trauma were formally acknowledged in the **Diagnostic and Statistical Manual of Mental Disorders (DSM-III)**, the authoritative text of American psychiatry.

This inclusion did not occur in a vacuum. It was the culmination of decades of clinical observation, survivor testimony, political struggle, and cultural shifts. While the Vietnam War provided the immediate impetus for the recognition of trauma-related syndromes, the intellectual and social foundations of PTSD as a diagnosis were laid earlier, in the experiences of war veterans, survivors of sexual violence, and children subjected to abuse.

This chapter examines the origins of PTSD as a diagnostic category, tracing its development from early concepts such as "shell shock" and "traumatic neurosis," through the advocacy of Vietnam veterans and feminist activists, to the debates within psychiatry that led to its formal recognition. The story of PTSD's origins is thus both a scientific and a political narrative, revealing how medical categories are shaped not only by evidence but also by the cultural and historical contexts in which they emerge.

Early Concepts of Trauma

Long before PTSD entered the psychiatric lexicon, clinicians struggled to describe the effects of overwhelming experiences.

- **19th Century: "Railway Spine" and Traumatic Neurosis**
  With the expansion of industrial transportation in the 19th century, physicians began documenting cases of individuals involved in railway accidents who reported chronic anxiety, nightmares, and startle responses. These syndromes were labeled "railway spine" or "traumatic neurosis," and though poorly understood, they foreshadowed later recognition of post-traumatic conditions.

- **World War I: Shell Shock**
  During the First World War, thousands of soldiers presented with tremors, paralysis, mutism, and other symptoms that could not be explained by physical injuries. Initially assumed to result from physical concussions due to exploding shells, the condition soon called "shell shock" was later recognized as a psychological response to overwhelming stress. Treatments varied widely, from rest and psychotherapy to punitive measures, reflecting ambivalence about whether the condition was a sign of injury or weakness.
- **World War II: Combat Fatigue and Gross Stress Reaction**
  By the Second World War, psychiatry had developed more sophisticated frameworks, labeling acute war-related symptoms as "combat fatigue." The DSM-I (1952) included "gross stress reaction" as a diagnosis, but this category assumed symptoms would resolve once the stressor was removed. When the DSM-II appeared in 1968, "gross stress reaction" was eliminated, leaving psychiatry without a diagnostic home for chronic trauma-related syndromes.

This historical backdrop is crucial: the absence of a diagnostic category in the late 1960s and 1970s meant that Vietnam veterans returning with long-term trauma symptoms were left without a recognized diagnosis. Their suffering fell into a psychiatric void.

The Vietnam Veterans and the Push for Recognition

As discussed in the previous chapter, Vietnam veterans experienced profound and enduring psychological distress. Their advocacy was critical in pressuring psychiatry to reconsider trauma as a legitimate category.

- **Veterans' Advocacy**: Groups such as Vietnam Veterans Against the War and grassroots "rap groups" created spaces where veterans could articulate shared experiences. These collective testimonies revealed strikingly consistent patterns of trauma symptoms, challenging the notion that they were isolated or idiosyncratic.
- **Clinical Observations**: Psychiatrists like Robert Jay Lifton and Chaim Shatan became outspoken advocates for veterans, publishing

influential articles that described the psychological aftermath of Vietnam as a coherent syndrome. Lifton's concept of the "survivor syndrome," initially applied to Hiroshima survivors, provided a conceptual bridge to understanding veterans' symptoms.

- **Political Pressure**: The visible suffering of veterans, combined with widespread public debate about the war, made it increasingly difficult for psychiatry to ignore trauma. The veterans' movement forced a reconsideration of earlier diagnostic frameworks that had minimized chronic post-combat conditions.

The veterans thus played a dual role: they were both patients and advocates, demanding recognition not only for themselves but also for trauma as a broader category of human experience.

Feminist Activism and the Expansion of Trauma

While veterans catalyzed one dimension of trauma recognition, feminist activism in the 1970s brought another critical set of voices into the discussion: survivors of **rape, domestic violence, and childhood abuse**.

- **Rape Trauma Syndrome**: In 1974, psychologists Ann Burgess and Lynda Holmstrom published their landmark study on "rape trauma syndrome," documenting the acute and long-term psychological consequences of sexual assault. Their work challenged the pervasive tendency to blame or disbelieve victims, reframing their experiences within a clinical, trauma-informed framework.
- **Domestic Violence Shelters**: The rise of women's shelters in the 1970s provided spaces where survivors of domestic abuse could share their experiences. These collective testimonies, much like the veterans' rap groups, revealed consistent patterns of trauma symptoms that transcended individual circumstances.
- **Child Abuse Recognition**: Pediatricians and child psychologists began to document the profound psychological and developmental consequences of childhood neglect and abuse. The 1960s and 1970s saw growing public recognition of child maltreatment, which in turn expanded psychiatry's awareness of trauma beyond the battlefield.

Feminist activists thus expanded the scope of trauma discourse, demonstrating that overwhelming experiences of helplessness, terror, and violation were not confined to soldiers but also pervaded domestic and everyday life. Their advocacy was instrumental in broadening the conceptual basis for PTSD.

The DSM-III and the Institutionalization of PTSD

The turning point came with the revision of the **DSM-III**, published in 1980. This edition introduced PTSD as a distinct diagnostic category, defined by clusters of symptoms that included intrusive recollections, avoidance, numbing, and hyperarousal.

- **The Committee Debates**: The DSM-III task force initially resisted including PTSD, fearing it would medicalize normal responses to stress. However, persistent lobbying by veterans' advocates, clinicians, and researchers eventually convinced the committee that the evidence justified a new diagnosis.
- **The Diagnostic Criteria**: PTSD was unique in that it explicitly linked symptoms to an external stressor an overwhelming event "outside the range of usual human experience." This marked a departure from other psychiatric diagnoses, which typically emphasized internal pathology rather than external causation.
- **The Political Dimension**: The inclusion of PTSD also reflected broader cultural shifts. By 1980, the U.S. was grappling with the legacies of Vietnam, the women's movement, and growing awareness of child abuse. PTSD crystallized these diverse experiences into a single diagnostic framework, giving them legitimacy within psychiatry.

The Broader Implications of PTSD

The inclusion of PTSD in the DSM-III had profound implications:

1. **Clinical Legitimacy**: Survivors could now receive a recognized diagnosis, opening pathways to treatment and disability benefits.
2. **Research Expansion**: PTSD became a focal point for research,

spurring studies in neuroscience, psychophysiology, and treatment efficacy.

3. **Cultural Awareness**: PTSD entered public discourse, shaping films, literature, and media representations of trauma.
4. **Policy Change**: Governments expanded funding for veteran services and began to recognize the public health burden of trauma.

Importantly, the PTSD diagnosis also carried limitations. By emphasizing extraordinary stressors "outside the range of usual human experience," it implicitly excluded chronic, everyday forms of trauma such as systemic racism, poverty, or emotional neglect. Later revisions would grapple with these limitations, but the initial inclusion nonetheless represented a vital step.

Conclusion

The origins of PTSD as a diagnosis reveal the interplay of science, advocacy, and politics. It was not simply the product of laboratory research or clinical observation but the outcome of survivors' struggles for recognition. Vietnam veterans, feminist activists, child advocates, and pioneering clinicians together forced psychiatry to confront trauma as a pervasive and enduring human reality.

The inclusion of PTSD in the DSM-III was thus both a scientific and a moral achievement. It validated the experiences of survivors who had long been silenced, and it laid the foundation for the revolutions in trauma research and treatment that would follow in subsequent decades.

In the next chapter, we will examine those revolutions more closely, tracing how the 1970s and 1980s witnessed a profound shift in psychiatry's understanding of trauma, fueled by survivor testimony, clinical innovation, and the rise of neuroscience.

CHAPTER THREE: HOW TRAUMA MANIFESTS AS FLASHBACKS, NIGHTMARES, AND EMOTIONAL NUMBNESS

Introduction

One of the most striking aspects of trauma is its persistence. Long after a traumatic event has ended, survivors often report that it continues to intrude into their daily lives through unwanted memories, dreams, and bodily sensations. These manifestations are not simply "bad memories" but vivid, involuntary re-experiences that resist conscious control.

Among the most widely documented symptoms of trauma are **flashbacks**, **nightmares**, and **emotional numbness**. Each represents a different way in which trauma alters the mind and body: flashbacks embody the sudden reliving of the past in the present; nightmares capture the haunting of sleep by trauma; and emotional numbness reflects the shutting down of affect as a defense against overwhelming pain.

This chapter examines how these symptoms arise, how they affect survivors, and what they reveal about the fundamental nature of traumatic memory. By exploring both clinical evidence and survivor testimony, we can see how trauma disrupts the ordinary processes of memory, emotion, and identity, leaving individuals trapped between a past they cannot forget and a present they cannot fully inhabit.

Flashbacks: The Past as Present

Flashbacks are perhaps the most dramatic expression of trauma. Survivors describe them as sudden, overwhelming experiences in which the traumatic event is not remembered but **re-lived**.

Characteristics of Flashbacks

- **Involuntary**: They arise without conscious intention, often triggered by sensory cues such as sounds, smells, or visual images.
- **Vividness**: Survivors report feeling as though they are back in the traumatic situation, with the same intensity of fear, pain, or

helplessness.

- **Loss of Time**: During a flashback, the distinction between past and present collapses. Individuals may react as though the trauma is happening again, shouting, ducking for cover, or dissociating.
- **Physiological Responses**: Flashbacks often include rapid heart rate, sweating, trembling, or a sense of impending doom, reflecting the activation of the body's fight-or-flight system.

Clinical Example

Vietnam veterans described flashbacks in which the sound of a helicopter or fireworks on the Fourth of July would transport them back to battlefields. Survivors of sexual assault have reported flashbacks triggered by particular scents or even seemingly benign touches. These reactions are not under conscious control but emerge from deep, automatic processes in the brain.

The Neurobiological Basis

Research in the late 20th century revealed that traumatic memories are encoded differently from ordinary memories.

- The **amygdala**, the brain's fear center, is hyperactive during trauma and imprints emotional intensity.
- The **hippocampus**, which normally situates memories in time and context, is disrupted, leading to fragmented and timeless recollections.
- The **prefrontal cortex**, responsible for rational regulation, is often underactive during trauma, preventing integration into narrative memory.

As a result, traumatic memories are stored as sensory fragments images, sounds, bodily sensations rather than coherent stories. Flashbacks represent the involuntary eruption of these fragments into consciousness.

Nightmares: Trauma in Sleep

If flashbacks dominate waking life, nightmares demonstrate how trauma invades the domain of sleep. Survivors often report recurring dreams that replay the traumatic event or symbolically represent its themes.

Common Features

- **Repetition**: Trauma nightmares are often repetitive, with the same scenes or variations recurring for years.
- **Intensity**: They provoke extreme fear, causing individuals to wake in panic, drenched in sweat, or unable to return to sleep.
- **Symbolism**: Some nightmares reproduce the trauma literally, while others depict it metaphorically, such as dreams of being chased, trapped, or attacked.

Consequences

Chronic nightmares disrupt restorative sleep, leading to fatigue, irritability, and cognitive difficulties. The fear of nightmares may also cause survivors to avoid sleep altogether, compounding psychological distress.

Clinical Example

Holocaust survivors often reported dreams of being hunted or trapped, decades after liberation. Children who experienced abuse frequently describe monsters or dark figures in their dreams, symbolic representations of their abusers.

Neurobiological Insights

Studies of sleep architecture show that trauma survivors often experience abnormalities in **REM sleep**, the stage associated with dreaming and memory consolidation. Normally, REM sleep helps integrate emotional experiences into long-term memory. In trauma, however, this process appears disrupted, leading to repetitive, unprocessed dreams that replay the event.

Emotional Numbness: The Silent Wound

While flashbacks and nightmares represent intrusive symptoms, emotional numbness reflects the opposite: the shutting down of emotional life. Survivors often describe feeling detached, hollow, or unable to experience joy, love, or intimacy.

Manifestations

- **Detachment from Others**: Survivors may feel estranged from loved ones, unable to connect emotionally.
- **Loss of Interest**: Activities that once brought pleasure no longer do.
- **Blunted Affect**: Emotions are flattened; survivors may describe

themselves as "robotic" or "dead inside."

- **Avoidance**: Emotional numbness often coexists with deliberate avoidance of trauma reminders, such as places, conversations, or media.

Adaptive Function

Paradoxically, emotional numbness can be understood as a defense mechanism. By shutting down overwhelming affect, the psyche protects itself from being flooded by terror or grief. However, this defense comes at the cost of vitality and connection.

Clinical Example

A veteran may avoid family gatherings because he feels unable to engage emotionally. A survivor of childhood abuse may struggle to form intimate relationships, fearing vulnerability. These patterns can perpetuate isolation and reinforce the sense of being fundamentally changed by trauma.

Neurobiological Mechanisms

Research suggests that emotional numbness involves hypoactivation of brain regions such as the **anterior cingulate cortex** and **prefrontal cortex**, which are involved in emotional awareness and regulation. Chronic activation of stress hormones like cortisol may also blunt emotional responsiveness over time.

Interplay of Symptoms

Flashbacks, nightmares, and emotional numbness do not exist in isolation. They interact in complex ways:

- Flashbacks and nightmares represent the **intrusion** of traumatic memory.
- Emotional numbness represents the **avoidance** of that memory.
- Survivors often oscillate between hyperarousal (flashbacks, nightmares) and hypoarousal (numbness), unable to achieve equilibrium.

This dynamic reflects the core paradox of trauma: the past is simultaneously **inescapable** and **unbearable**. Survivors are caught between relentless intrusion and desperate avoidance, both of which disrupt ordinary life.

Broader Implications

Understanding these symptoms has profound implications:

- **Clinical Practice**: Recognition of flashbacks, nightmares, and numbness as trauma-specific symptoms was critical to the PTSD diagnosis.
- **Survivor Validation**: Naming these experiences as trauma manifestations reduces stigma and offers survivors a language to articulate suffering.
- **Neuroscience of Memory**: Trauma research has reshaped our understanding of memory as not merely cognitive but deeply embodied, fragmented, and emotional.

Conclusion

Flashbacks, nightmares, and emotional numbness exemplify how trauma disrupts the ordinary functions of memory, sleep, and affect. They demonstrate that trauma is not simply remembered but re-lived, not simply an event in the past but an ongoing presence in the psyche and body.

These manifestations also underscore the central paradox of trauma: the mind cannot fully assimilate overwhelming experience, leaving survivors trapped in cycles of intrusion and avoidance. Recognizing these patterns was essential to the development of PTSD as a diagnosis and continues to guide treatment approaches today.

In the next chapter, we will explore the **Revolutions in Understanding Trauma** during the 1970s and 1980s, examining how psychiatry shifted from dismissing trauma as weakness to recognizing it as a profound alteration of the brain and mind.

CHAPTER FOUR: REVOLUTIONS IN UNDERSTANDING TRAUMA

Introduction

The late 1970s and 1980s marked a **paradigm shift** in psychiatry's approach to trauma. What had once been regarded as a marginal, even controversial, set of symptoms came to occupy the center of psychiatric inquiry. This revolution did not occur spontaneously. It was driven by an intersection of **patient advocacy, clinical innovation, feminist critique, and neuroscientific discovery**, all converging to transform how the mental health community conceptualized trauma.

This chapter explores the intellectual and cultural revolution that occurred in this period, focusing on:

1. The shift in psychiatry's frameworks from psychodynamic interpretations to empirically grounded diagnostic categories.
2. The central role of **patient narratives** particularly those of Vietnam veterans and survivors of sexual violence in forcing psychiatry to confront trauma as a legitimate condition.
3. The beginnings of **neuroscience-based research**, which provided biological explanations for trauma and gave the diagnosis scientific credibility.

This chapter demonstrates that the transformation of trauma studies was not simply a matter of new data, but a profound reorientation in medicine's relationship to suffering.

From Psychodynamic Theories to Diagnostic Psychiatry

For much of the 20th century, psychiatry was dominated by **psychoanalysis**, which viewed traumatic symptoms as the result of unconscious conflicts rather than responses to external events.

- **Freudian Legacy**: Early in his career, Freud linked hysteria to sexual trauma, but later abandoned this position, favoring theories of internal drives and fantasies. This shift marginalized the role of external trauma in psychiatric thought.
- **Mid-20th Century Psychiatry**: By the 1950s and 1960s, trauma-related syndromes had been largely relegated to the background. Diagnoses such as "combat fatigue" or "gross stress reaction" were considered temporary, and the DSM-II (1968) omitted trauma entirely.

The **publication of the DSM-III in 1980** revolutionized psychiatry by shifting toward **descriptive, symptom-based criteria** rather than psychoanalytic theories. Within this new framework, **PTSD was institutionalized**, legitimizing trauma as a diagnostic entity and shifting the focus from speculation about unconscious motives to observable, reportable symptoms.

Patient Stories as Catalysts

A central driver of this revolution was the **testimony of survivors**. Their narratives forced psychiatry to acknowledge what had long been ignored.

Veterans' Testimonies

- Vietnam veterans described vivid flashbacks, hypervigilance, and emotional withdrawal symptoms that did not conform to existing psychiatric categories.
- In rap groups and therapeutic collectives, veterans documented patterns of suffering that clinicians could not dismiss as idiosyncratic.

Women's Voices

- Survivors of rape and domestic violence broke longstanding silences.

Feminist activism reframed these experiences not as private shame but as systemic violence with lasting psychological effects.

- The recognition of "rape trauma syndrome" by Burgess and Holmstrom (1974) provided empirical evidence that sexual assault produced predictable psychological consequences.

Childhood Trauma

- Growing awareness of child abuse fueled by social movements and new research expanded the scope of trauma discourse. Children's testimonies revealed how trauma in formative years had profound, long-term consequences for development.

Patient stories challenged psychiatry to **listen**. They revealed that trauma was not an aberration confined to battlefields, but a pervasive human experience with consistent psychological patterns.

The Scientific Reorientation

While survivor narratives provided the moral and political impetus, **scientific developments** provided psychiatry with the tools to translate these experiences into medical legitimacy.

Early Psychophysiology

Studies of trauma survivors in the 1970s revealed measurable alterations in arousal and stress response:

- Elevated heart rates, exaggerated startle responses, and disrupted sleep patterns.
- Hyperactivity of the autonomic nervous system, consistent with ongoing activation of fight-or-flight mechanisms.

These findings challenged the idea that trauma symptoms were purely psychological, demonstrating that they had measurable biological correlates.

Brain Imaging and Neuroscience

By the 1980s, emerging neuroimaging technologies allowed researchers to examine the brain's role in trauma. Early studies suggested:

- The **amygdala** played a central role in exaggerated fear responses.

- The **hippocampus** showed abnormalities related to fragmented memory.
- The **prefrontal cortex** appeared less active during traumatic recall, suggesting impaired regulation of emotional responses.

These discoveries reframed trauma not as weakness or moral failing but as a **biological injury** to neural circuits regulating memory, fear, and emotion.

The Cultural Context of the 1970s–80s

The revolutions in trauma understanding were inseparable from their cultural moment.

- **Post-Vietnam America**: The U.S. was grappling with a controversial war and the visible suffering of its veterans. PTSD provided a language for their pain.
- **The Women's Movement**: Feminist critiques exposed how psychiatry had historically silenced women's testimonies of violence. Their activism forced the medical establishment to confront sexual and domestic trauma.
- **Child Protection Movements**: Rising awareness of child abuse and neglect provided further evidence of trauma's widespread impact.

Together, these movements created a **moral imperative** that psychiatry could not ignore.

Resistance and Controversy

Not all psychiatrists welcomed the new focus on trauma. Critics argued that:

- PTSD risked **pathologizing normal responses** to adversity.
- The criteria were overly broad, potentially medicalizing political and social suffering.
- Some feared the diagnosis would be used for **secondary gain** (e.g., disability claims by veterans).

Despite these debates, the legitimacy of PTSD grew steadily, supported by the convergence of survivor advocacy, clinical evidence, and neuroscience.

Legacy of the 1970s–80s Trauma Revolution

The transformations of this period left enduring legacies:

1. **Integration into Psychiatry**: Trauma became a central concern, reshaping diagnostic manuals, treatment approaches, and research agendas.
2. **Public Awareness**: PTSD entered popular culture, influencing media, literature, and public policy.
3. **Foundations for Neuroscience**: Early imaging and psychophysiological studies paved the way for today's sophisticated understanding of trauma's effects on the brain.
4. **Ethical Shifts**: Psychiatry began to take survivor testimony seriously, breaking with a history of silencing or pathologizing such accounts.

Conclusion

The 1970s and 1980s marked a **revolutionary era** in trauma studies. Survivors' voices, combined with scientific advances, overturned decades of neglect and denial. Psychiatry shifted from dismissing trauma as weakness or hysteria to recognizing it as a legitimate condition with biological, psychological, and social dimensions.

This revolution laid the groundwork for the next stage of inquiry: the exploration of how trauma reshapes the brain itself. In the next chapter, we will examine the **early neuroscience of trauma**, focusing on how brain-imaging studies revealed that trauma literally rewires the circuits of fear, stress, and memory.

CHAPTER FIVE: LOOKING INTO THE BRAIN – NEUROSCIENCE OF TRAUMA

Introduction

By the late 20th century, the recognition of trauma as a psychiatric diagnosis had transformed both clinical practice and cultural understanding. Yet, one crucial question remained: **how does trauma alter the brain itself?**

The advent of modern neuroscience in the 1980s and 1990s offered unprecedented tools to answer this question. Using brain-imaging technologies, psychophysiological studies, and neuroendocrinological assays, researchers began to reveal that trauma is not simply a psychological wound but a **biological injury** that reshapes neural circuits governing fear, memory, and self-regulation.

This chapter traces the **early neuroscience of trauma**, beginning with the first psychophysiological studies of veterans, moving through the pioneering brain-imaging research of the 1990s, and concluding with the discovery that trauma can permanently rewire stress and fear circuits. In doing so, it illustrates how neuroscience not only validated survivors' experiences but also redefined trauma as a disorder of the entire mind–body system.

Psychophysiological Foundations

Before the widespread use of brain imaging, researchers turned to **psychophysiology** to measure the body's responses to trauma.

Early Findings in Veterans

Studies of Vietnam veterans in the late 1970s and early 1980s showed that:

- Veterans with trauma histories exhibited **exaggerated startle responses** when exposed to sudden sounds.
- Their heart rates, blood pressure, and galvanic skin responses spiked dramatically in response to trauma-related cues.
- These reactions occurred even when veterans consciously denied emotional responses, suggesting that trauma operated on **automatic, non-conscious pathways**.

Implications

These findings demonstrated that trauma was not simply "in the mind." It was deeply **embodied**, activating the autonomic nervous system and stress hormones long after the danger had passed. Trauma, in other words, left a lasting physiological imprint.

The Rise of Brain Imaging

The 1990s brought a new era in psychiatry: the widespread use of **functional brain imaging** technologies, such as positron emission tomography (PET) and functional magnetic resonance imaging (fMRI). For the first time, researchers could visualize trauma's effects on the living brain.

Key Discoveries

1. **Hyperactive Amygdala**
    - The amygdala, a small almond-shaped structure deep in the temporal lobe, was found to be overactive in trauma survivors.
    - This explained why survivors remained in states of **hypervigilance** and exaggerated fear, even in safe environments.
2. **Hypoactive Prefrontal Cortex**
    - The medial prefrontal cortex, crucial for regulating emotions and suppressing fear responses, showed reduced activity.
    - This imbalance meant survivors were **less able to inhibit amygdala-driven fear**, leading to persistent hyperarousal and intrusive symptoms.
3. **Hippocampal Dysfunction**
    - The hippocampus, essential for contextualizing memory, often showed reduced volume in trauma survivors.
    - This provided a neurological basis for **fragmented, timeless traumatic memories**, where the event feels as though it is happening in the present.

Clinical Implications

Together, these discoveries provided a neurobiological explanation for the "triad" of trauma symptoms:

- **Intrusion** (flashbacks, nightmares) → amygdala hyperactivity.
- **Avoidance/numbing** → prefrontal hypoactivity.
- **Fragmented memory** → hippocampal dysfunction.

The Stress Hormone System

Parallel to brain imaging studies, researchers explored the role of **stress hormones**, particularly cortisol and adrenaline, in trauma.

Dysregulation of Cortisol

- Normally, cortisol helps regulate stress responses, rising in the face of danger and falling when safety returns.
- In trauma survivors, studies found paradoxical patterns: some exhibited **chronically low cortisol**, suggesting the system had become exhausted from overuse.

Elevated Adrenaline

- Trauma survivors often displayed heightened levels of norepinephrine (a form of adrenaline).
- This explained the **hyperarousal, irritability, and sleep disturbances** common in PTSD.

The Body Remembers

These hormonal patterns demonstrated that trauma is not merely "remembered" cognitively. It is **encoded in the body's stress systems**, which continue to react as if the trauma is ongoing.

Trauma as Rewiring of Brain Circuits

By the early 2000s, a consensus was emerging: trauma does not simply disrupt psychological well-being; it **rewires the fundamental circuits of survival.**

Fear Circuits

- Hyperactive amygdala + hypoactive prefrontal cortex → a brain primed for danger.
- Survivors interpret ambiguous cues as threatening, perpetuating cycles of fear and hypervigilance.

Memory Circuits

- Reduced hippocampal function prevents integration of traumatic experiences into coherent narratives.
- Instead of being stored as past events, traumatic fragments return as present-tense intrusions.

Self-Regulation Circuits

- Altered connections between the prefrontal cortex and limbic system undermine the ability to regulate emotion.
- This leads to mood swings, irritability, dissociation, or shutdown (emotional numbness).

Validation of Survivor Experience

One of the most important consequences of trauma neuroscience was **validation**. Survivors who had long been told their symptoms were imaginary, exaggerated, or signs of weakness now had objective evidence: trauma changed the brain.

- Veterans could point to brain scans showing amygdala hyperactivity.
- Survivors of abuse could explain their fragmented memories as neurological, not moral failings.
- Clinicians gained powerful tools to counter stigma and justify treatment.

This scientific validation helped destigmatize trauma, integrating it into the broader framework of medicine and public health.

Limits and Critiques

Despite its advances, trauma neuroscience faced several critiques:

- **Reductionism**: Some argued that focusing on the brain risked ignoring social, cultural, and relational dimensions of trauma.
- **Ethical Issues**: Early studies often relied on exposing survivors to distressing stimuli, raising questions about retraumatization.
- **Over-Pathologizing**: Critics warned against medicalizing normal responses to adversity.

Nevertheless, the overall trajectory was clear: neuroscience profoundly deepened our understanding of trauma as a mind–body phenomenon.

Conclusion

The early neuroscience of trauma revealed that traumatic experience leaves **enduring imprints on the brain and body**. Through psychophysiology, brain imaging, and hormone research, scientists demonstrated that trauma disrupts fear regulation, memory integration, and stress systems.

These discoveries transformed trauma from a contested psychiatric diagnosis into a **neurobiological reality**. They not only validated survivor testimony but also paved the way for novel treatments aimed at rewiring the brain and restoring regulation.

CHAPTER SIX: THE ANATOMY OF SURVIVAL

Introduction

Trauma is, at its core, a disruption of survival. The very systems that evolved to protect the human organism those that enable rapid mobilization in the face of threat can become dysregulated and maladaptive when exposed to overwhelming danger. To understand trauma, one must therefore begin with the **neurobiology of survival**: the intricate interplay of brain structures, neural circuits, and bodily responses that mediate the "fight, flight, or freeze" reactions.

This chapter examines:

1. The **evolutionary roots of survival responses** and their adaptive value.
2. The **neuroanatomical foundations** of trauma, with emphasis on the amygdala, hippocampus, and prefrontal cortex.
3. The **fight, flight, freeze** model and its relevance to trauma symptomatology.
4. The transformation of survival circuits from protective mechanisms into sources of chronic dysregulation.

By mapping the anatomy of survival, we gain critical insight into how trauma leaves a biological imprint, shaping perception, behavior, and selfhood long after the original threat has passed.

Evolutionary Logic of Survival Responses

All organisms are equipped with mechanisms to detect danger and mobilize defenses. For humans, these mechanisms are embedded in **ancient neural structures** shared across species.

- **Fight**: When escape is impossible, the body prepares for confrontation. Muscles tense, heart rate accelerates, and adrenaline floods the system.
- **Flight**: When avoidance is possible, energy is diverted toward escape.

- **Freeze**: When danger is overwhelming and neither fight nor flight is viable, the body immobilizes. This response may conserve energy and reduce detection by predators.

These responses are orchestrated largely outside conscious awareness, reflecting the **primacy of survival over cognition**. From an evolutionary standpoint, survival circuits operate on the principle of speed: it is better to react instantly to a potential threat than to deliberate and risk annihilation.

The Amygdala: Sentinel of Threat

The **amygdala** serves as the brain's alarm system. Located deep in the medial temporal lobe, it continuously scans sensory input for signs of danger.

Functions in Survival

- **Rapid threat detection**: The amygdala can trigger defensive responses milliseconds before conscious recognition.
- **Emotional memory encoding**: Events associated with fear are stored with heightened salience, ensuring that future threats are rapidly recognized.
- **Autonomic activation**: The amygdala signals the hypothalamus to release stress hormones, priming the body for fight or flight.

Trauma and Amygdala Hyperactivity

In trauma survivors, imaging studies consistently show **amygdala hyperactivation**:

- Neutral stimuli are misinterpreted as threatening.
- The system becomes hypersensitive, responding as if danger is omnipresent.
- This underlies symptoms of **hypervigilance, exaggerated startle, and intrusive flashbacks**.

The amygdala thus illustrates how trauma is not merely remembered it is relived at the level of neurocircuitry.

The Hippocampus: Keeper of Context

If the amygdala is the sentinel of threat, the **hippocampus** provides the context in which experiences are situated.

Normal Function

- Encodes episodic memories (the "where" and "when" of events).
- Differentiates between present and past, safety and danger.
- Communicates with the prefrontal cortex to regulate fear based on context.

Trauma and Hippocampal Impairment

- Many studies report **reduced hippocampal volume** in trauma survivors.
- Impaired contextualization means traumatic memories are stored as **fragments** sensations, images, or bodily states rather than coherent narratives.
- This explains why trauma survivors experience flashbacks as though they are happening "now," rather than recalling them as events from the past.

The hippocampus thus mediates the distinction between past threat and present safety a distinction often lost in trauma.

The Prefrontal Cortex: Regulator of Reason

The **prefrontal cortex (PFC)**, particularly its medial regions, is essential for regulating survival responses.

Roles in Regulation

- **Inhibits amygdala activity**, dampening excessive fear responses.
- Integrates rational appraisal with emotional signals.
- Supports decision-making and impulse control.

Trauma and Prefrontal Hypoactivity

- Imaging studies show **reduced PFC activity** in trauma survivors, especially during exposure to trauma reminders.
- Without adequate regulation, the amygdala dominates, producing persistent hyperarousal and intrusive symptoms.
- Survivors often describe feeling as though their "rational brain shuts down" when triggered a description consistent with neuroimaging findings.

The breakdown of amygdale PFC balance exemplifies the **core dysregulation of trauma**: unchecked fear without effective cognitive control.

The Freeze Response and Dissociation

While fight and flight are widely recognized, the **freeze response** deserves equal attention.

Neurobiology of Freeze

- Involves activation of the **periaqueductal gray (PAG)** in the midbrain.
- Produces immobilization, analgesia, and a sense of detachment.
- Serves as a last-resort survival strategy when escape or defense is impossible.

Clinical Manifestations

- Survivors often report feelings of **numbness, depersonalization, or dissociation** during trauma.
- In chronic form, dissociation becomes a protective strategy, but one

that fragments memory and disrupts integration.

The freeze response illustrates how survival mechanisms can, under conditions of overwhelming trauma, become maladaptive sources of long-term psychopathology.

Chronic Dysregulation of Survival Circuits

When survival responses are repeatedly activated without resolution, the brain undergoes **neuroplastic changes** that entrench trauma symptoms.

- **Amygdala sensitization**: Thresholds for fear responses are lowered.
- **Hippocampal shrinkage**: Contextual memory becomes impaired, reinforcing flashbacks.
- **PFC weakening**: Regulatory capacity diminishes over time.

The result is a brain that is **primed for threat detection**, even in environments of safety. Trauma survivors live in a state of perpetual readiness for danger, often at immense psychological and physiological cost.

Clinical Implications

Understanding the anatomy of survival has profound clinical consequences:

1. **Validation**: Symptoms such as hypervigilance, flashbacks, and dissociation reflect biological dysregulation, not weakness of character.
2. **Treatment Targets**: Effective interventions must address not only cognition but also **neural circuits and bodily states**.
3. **Prevention**: Early intervention after trauma may prevent survival circuits from becoming entrenched in maladaptive patterns.

Conclusion

The anatomy of survival reveals how trauma commandeers ancient biological systems designed to protect life. The amygdala's vigilance, the hippocampus's contextualization, the prefrontal cortex's regulation, and the freeze response's immobilization all represent adaptive functions. Yet, when overwhelmed, these systems can lock survivors into cycles of fear, dissociation, and dysregulation.

Trauma thus demonstrates a paradox: the very mechanisms that evolved to preserve life can, under conditions of extremity, perpetuate suffering. Recognizing this paradox is essential for both scientific understanding and clinical practice.

In the next chapter, we turn from the brain's survival anatomy to the **body brain connections**, examining how trauma is not only encoded in neural circuits but also inscribed in the physiology of the body itself.

CHAPTER SEVEN: BODY BRAIN CONNECTIONS

Introduction

Trauma does not reside solely in the mind; it is embodied. Survivors frequently describe their trauma not only in terms of thoughts and memories but also as sensations: a pounding heart, a tight chest, shallow breathing, or an inexplicable sense of dread. These bodily imprints are not secondary to the psychological impact of trauma they are intrinsic to it.

Over the past three decades, research has increasingly revealed that trauma is a disorder of **body brain integration**. Stress hormones, autonomic responses, and muscular patterns of tension form part of trauma's legacy. The body becomes a repository of traumatic memory, carrying experiences that the conscious mind may seek to avoid or repress.

This chapter explores:

1. The **embodied nature of traumatic memory**.
2. The role of **stress hormones** in perpetuating trauma.
3. The physiology of the **autonomic nervous system** and its dysregulation.
4. The evidence that trauma symptoms are as much somatic as they are cognitive.

By tracing these connections, we gain a deeper appreciation for the inseparability of body and brain in the aftermath of overwhelming experience.

Trauma as Stored Bodily Memory

The concept that the body "remembers" trauma long predates modern neuroscience. Survivors often report involuntary bodily responses to triggers long before conscious recall.

Clinical Observations

- Veterans may drop to the ground upon hearing fireworks, even if they consciously know they are safe.
- Survivors of assault may feel visceral nausea or muscle tension when confronted with reminders of the event.
- Many report a **sense of reliving trauma through the body** heart pounding, sweating, shaking even when the memory remains fragmented.

These observations suggest that trauma memory is not merely stored in declarative (narrative) systems but also in **procedural and sensory systems.**

Neurobiological Basis

- The amygdala encodes fear associations linked to bodily states.
- The hippocampus, impaired by trauma, fails to integrate these sensations into a coherent past narrative.
- As a result, traumatic experiences are reactivated **as sensations**, not as recollections.

This phenomenon explains why survivors often say, "I don't remember it, but my body does."

Stress Hormones and Their Lasting Effects

The **hypothalamic pituitary adrenal (HPA) axis** orchestrates the hormonal response to stress. Trauma fundamentally alters this system.

Cortisol Dysregulation

- In acute stress, cortisol mobilizes energy and dampens inflammation.
- In chronic trauma, cortisol patterns often become dysregulated some survivors exhibit persistently **low cortisol**, while others display heightened or erratic levels.
- Low cortisol may paradoxically **increase vulnerability** to stress, as the system loses flexibility in response.

Norepinephrine and Hyperarousal

- Elevated norepinephrine (adrenaline) is common among trauma survivors.
- This produces symptoms of **hypervigilance, insomnia, irritability, and exaggerated startle responses**.
- It also contributes to the strengthening of traumatic memories, since norepinephrine enhances consolidation of emotionally charged events.

Long-Term Consequences

Chronic dysregulation of stress hormones contributes to:

- Cardiovascular disease.
- Autoimmune and inflammatory disorders.
- Metabolic disturbances.

Thus, trauma is not only a mental health issue but a **major public health burden** with systemic bodily consequences.

Autonomic Nervous System Dysregulation

The **autonomic nervous system (ANS)**, consisting of the sympathetic ("fight/flight") and parasympathetic ("rest/digest") branches, is central to trauma's imprint.

Sympathetic Dominance

- Trauma survivors often display persistent sympathetic arousal: elevated heart rate, shallow breathing, muscle tension.
- This contributes to chronic anxiety, sleep disruption, and heightened startle responses.

Parasympathetic Collapse

- In contrast, the **freeze/dissociative response** involves parasympathetic overactivation, mediated by the vagus nerve.
- This produces states of immobilization, numbness, or detachment.

Polyvagal Theory

Stephen Porges' **polyvagal theory** has provided a framework for understanding trauma as involving shifts between different autonomic states:

- **Ventral vagal system** → social engagement, calmness.
- **Sympathetic activation** → mobilization for fight/flight.
- **Dorsal vagal shutdown** → immobilization, dissociation.

Trauma survivors often oscillate between hyperarousal and shutdown, with limited capacity to sustain regulated states of engagement.

Somatic Expressions of Trauma

Trauma often manifests as bodily symptoms without obvious medical cause:

- Chronic pain syndromes (fibromyalgia, tension headaches).
- Gastrointestinal disturbances (irritable bowel syndrome).
- Sleep disturbances and fatigue.
- Musculoskeletal rigidity, particularly in the neck, shoulders, and jaw.

These symptoms reflect not imagined illness but the physiological consequences of dysregulated survival systems.

Clinical Example

A survivor of childhood abuse may present with chronic back pain and gastrointestinal complaints. Medical workups yield no structural pathology. Yet psychophysiological testing reveals elevated baseline muscle tension, heightened cortisol fluctuations, and exaggerated startle responses clear evidence of trauma's bodily imprint.

Trauma, Memory, and the Body

The distinction between **explicit memory** (conscious, narrative) and **implicit memory** (non-conscious, bodily) is crucial for understanding trauma.

- **Explicit memory** relies heavily on the hippocampus and prefrontal cortex.
- **Implicit memory** is mediated by subcortical systems (amygdala, cerebellum, brainstem) and expressed as bodily states, habits, or reflexes.

Trauma disrupts explicit memory, leaving survivors with fragmented recall. Yet implicit memory persists vividly in the body. This explains why therapies that target bodily regulation such as yoga, somatic experiencing, or neurofeedback can be effective when words alone fail.

Clinical Implications

1. **Trauma Is Embodied**
    - Symptoms such as muscle tension, digestive issues, and chronic pain reflect genuine neurobiological dysregulation.
    - Clinicians must attend to bodily symptoms, not dismiss them as "psychosomatic."
2. **Treatment Must Include the Body**
    - Interventions that engage the body (breathing practices, movement therapies, sensory grounding) complement cognitive approaches.
    - Integration of mind and body is essential for lasting recovery.
3. **Prevention of Chronic Illness**
    - By recognizing trauma's physiological imprint, clinicians can intervene earlier to reduce long-term health consequences.

Conclusion

Trauma is not confined to the brain's higher functions of thought and memory. It reverberates through the body's stress systems, autonomic circuits, and hormonal regulation. Survivors live with bodies that "remember" danger, often in ways that defy conscious awareness.

The recognition of trauma as embodied reshapes both science and therapy. It underscores why recovery must involve not only talking about trauma but also **working through it in the body**.

In the next chapter, we turn to **developmental trauma**, examining how early neglect and abuse fundamentally alter both body and brain, shaping lifelong patterns of attachment, regulation, and vulnerability.

CHAPTER EIGHT: DEVELOPMENTAL TRAUMA

Introduction

While acute trauma such as combat, natural disasters, or accidents can profoundly affect the human psyche, the trauma that occurs **within development itself** exerts even more pervasive and enduring consequences. Developmental trauma refers to the cumulative impact of **chronic neglect, abuse, or attachment disruption during childhood**, particularly during critical windows of neurological and emotional growth.

Unlike single-incident trauma, developmental trauma is not a rupture in an otherwise stable life course. It is woven into the very fabric of growth, shaping how the child's brain organizes itself, how relationships are internalized, and how the sense of self is constructed. Survivors often enter adulthood not only with the scars of specific events but with **fundamentally altered systems of regulation, attachment, and identity formation**.

This chapter examines:

1. The **nature and definition of developmental trauma**.
2. The **impact of early neglect and abuse** on brain development.
3. The role of **attachment disruptions** in shaping emotional regulation.
4. The long-term consequences across domains of mental, physical, and relational health.
5. Clinical implications for recognizing and addressing developmental trauma.

Defining Developmental Trauma

The term **developmental trauma** has gained prominence in recent decades, largely through the work of clinicians and researchers who found that many children did not fit neatly within the criteria for PTSD. These children often exhibited:

- Difficulty with attention and learning.
- Problems with impulse control and aggression.
- Heightened anxiety or emotional numbing.
- Deep-seated shame, worthlessness, or identity confusion.

Such patterns suggested a **complex, developmental form of trauma** distinct from adult-onset PTSD.

Developmental Trauma Disorder (DTD)

Though not yet formally included in the DSM, the proposal for **Developmental Trauma Disorder** highlights the need for diagnostic categories that capture:

- Dysregulation of affect and impulse.
- Disturbances in attention, cognition, and consciousness.
- Somatic distress and health problems.
- Profound relational difficulties.

DTD reflects the recognition that **chronic trauma during sensitive developmental periods leaves an imprint at every level of functioning.**

Early Neglect and Abuse: Impact on the Brain

The human brain is exquisitely sensitive to its environment during development. Early experiences literally sculpt neural architecture. When a child grows in a context of love and safety, neural networks supporting regulation and social connection flourish. In contrast, chronic abuse or neglect wires the brain for **survival, not growth**.

Amygdala and Hypervigilance

- Children exposed to early trauma often display an **enlarged or hyperactive amygdala**.
- This produces heightened sensitivity to threat, even in safe environments.
- It manifests behaviorally as anxiety, aggression, or avoidance.

Hippocampus and Memory

- Early trauma is associated with **reduced hippocampal volume**, impairing contextual memory.
- This contributes to fragmented recollections, learning difficulties, and problems distinguishing present safety from past threat.

Prefrontal Cortex and Regulation

- Chronic stress disrupts maturation of the **prefrontal cortex**, critical for impulse control and planning.
- As a result, children may struggle with attention, self-regulation, and executive functioning.

Stress Hormone Imbalance

- Repeated activation of the **HPA axis** leads to cortisol dysregulation.
- Long-term effects include vulnerability to depression, metabolic disorders, and immune dysfunction.

In sum, abuse and neglect alter brain development in ways that predispose to lifelong difficulties in regulation, learning, and health.

Attachment Disruptions and Emotional Regulation

Attachment theory, pioneered by John Bowlby, emphasized the necessity of secure caregiver–child bonds for healthy development. Trauma within these bonds produces not only fear of external dangers but also fear of the very people meant to provide protection.

Secure vs. Insecure Attachment

- **Secure attachment** provides a foundation for emotional regulation, resilience, and exploration.
- **Insecure attachment** (avoidant, ambivalent, disorganized) arises when caregivers are inconsistent, rejecting, or frightening.

Disorganized Attachment and Trauma

- In cases of abuse or neglect, the caregiver becomes both the source of comfort and the source of fear.
- This paradox produces **disorganized attachment**, characterized by contradictory behaviors, confusion, and lack of coherent strategies for seeking safety.
- In adulthood, this manifests as difficulties in trust, intimacy, and self-regulation.

Emotional Dysregulation

- Without reliable external regulation from caregivers, children cannot internalize the ability to soothe themselves.
- Emotional states oscillate between extremes rage, despair, numbness without modulation.

- This dysregulation underlies many later disorders, from borderline personality disorder to substance use.

Long-Term Consequences of Developmental Trauma

The imprint of developmental trauma extends across the lifespan. Survivors face elevated risks in nearly every domain of functioning.

Psychological Consequences

- Mood and anxiety disorders.
- Dissociation and identity disturbances.
- Complex PTSD and personality disorders.

Physical Health Consequences

- Adverse Childhood Experiences (ACEs) studies show a graded relationship between trauma exposure and risk of:
    - Cardiovascular disease.
    - Diabetes.
    - Chronic pain syndromes.
    - Early mortality.

Relational Consequences

- Difficulty forming stable, trusting relationships.
- Cycles of revictimization or abusive dynamics.
- Isolation and impaired parenting, perpetuating intergenerational trauma.

Developmental trauma thus functions not only as an individual tragedy but as a **societal challenge with intergenerational effects**.

Clinical Vignette

Consider a child raised in a household of neglect and intermittent violence. From an early age, the child learns that expressing needs is dangerous and that safety is unpredictable. By adolescence, the child struggles with explosive anger, difficulty concentrating, and chronic feelings of worthlessness. In adulthood, relationships remain unstable, and physical health begins to deteriorate due to stress-related illness.

This vignette illustrates how developmental trauma is not a discrete event but a **trajectory** one that shapes the arc of a life unless interrupted by intervention and healing.

Clinical Implications

1. **Recognition Beyond PTSD**
    - Many survivors of developmental trauma do not meet criteria for "classic" PTSD.
    - Clinicians must recognize broader patterns of dysregulation and relational disturbance.
2. **Treatment Must Address Attachment and Regulation**
    - Interventions must go beyond symptom reduction to foster new experiences of safety and connection.
    - Therapies such as attachment-based approaches, somatic therapies, and relationally focused interventions are vital.
3. **Early Intervention Is Crucial**
    - Preventing the entrenchment of developmental trauma requires **supporting caregivers, schools, and communities.**
    - Trauma-informed systems can mitigate long-term consequences.

Conclusion

Developmental trauma reshapes the brain, body, and psyche at the most fundamental levels. When abuse, neglect, or disrupted attachment occurs during critical windows of development, the child grows not in the soil of safety but in the terrain of survival. This produces enduring patterns of dysregulation, mistrust, and vulnerability to illness.

To address developmental trauma is to recognize that trauma is not only about discrete events but about the **absence of what is needed for healthy growth**. Healing, therefore, requires not only alleviating symptoms but cultivating new relational and bodily experiences that restore safety and regulation.

In the next part of the book, we shift focus from the adult and developmental neurobiology of trauma to **the minds of children** more directly, exploring how trauma manifests during childhood, how it shapes identity, and why society has long overlooked its prevalence.

CHAPTER NINE: THE HIDDEN EPIDEMIC OF CHILDHOOD TRAUMA

Introduction

Childhood trauma is both pervasive and profoundly underestimated. Although war, natural disasters, and interpersonal violence capture public attention, the far more common yet less visible traumas of **child abuse, neglect, and household dysfunction** shape the lives of millions each year. These experiences leave an enduring imprint on brain development, health, and social functioning.

Despite decades of evidence, society has been reluctant to fully acknowledge the scope of childhood trauma. This reluctance stems in part from denial society resists confronting the reality that many children suffer not at the hands of strangers but within their own homes. Moreover, children rarely have the voice or power to bring their suffering into public view.

This chapter will examine:

1. The **scope of childhood trauma** through epidemiological data.
2. Societal and cultural **blind spots** that perpetuate silence.
3. The **Adverse Childhood Experiences (ACE) studies** as a landmark in understanding long-term consequences.
4. The broader implications of childhood trauma as a **public health crisis.**

The Scope of Childhood Trauma

Childhood trauma encompasses a broad range of adverse experiences, including physical abuse, sexual abuse, emotional maltreatment, neglect, and exposure to domestic violence. In addition, living in environments characterized by substance abuse, parental mental illness, or criminal behavior increases vulnerability.

Global Prevalence

- The **World Health Organization** estimates that **up to 1 billion children** worldwide experience physical, sexual, or emotional violence each year.

- In the United States, the **Centers for Disease Control and Prevention (CDC)** reports that about **1 in 7 children** experiences abuse or neglect annually.
- Underreporting remains pervasive: many cases never come to the attention of authorities, meaning official statistics likely underestimate the true prevalence.

Everyday Traumas

While catastrophic events such as natural disasters and war gain visibility, the traumas most damaging to children are often chronic, hidden, and interpersonal. A child repeatedly neglected, belittled, or exposed to volatile caregiving experiences trauma no less real than the soldier in combat though it may be less easily recognized.

Societal Blind Spots

Despite its scope, childhood trauma has historically remained marginalized in public discourse.

Cultural Denial

- Societies often perpetuate myths that childhood is inherently safe or innocent.
- Abuse within the family challenges deep-seated cultural ideals of the home as a sanctuary, leading to minimization or denial.

Professional Blind Spots

- For decades, psychiatry and psychology focused more on adult pathology than on children's lived experiences.
- Symptoms of traumatized children were often misdiagnosed as conduct disorder, ADHD, or oppositional defiance, without recognition of their roots in trauma.

Stigma and Silence

- Survivors of childhood trauma face stigma when disclosing their histories.

- Shame and secrecy are compounded by fears of not being believed, particularly in cases of sexual abuse.

These blind spots perpetuate cycles of neglect in healthcare, education, and policy.

The ACE Studies: A Landmark in Trauma Research

In the 1990s, Vincent Felitti and colleagues conducted the **Adverse Childhood Experiences (ACE) Study**, which remains one of the most influential epidemiological investigations of trauma.

Methodology

- Over **17,000 participants**, largely middle-class and insured, were surveyed about exposure to ten categories of adversity, including abuse, neglect, and household dysfunction.
- Their histories were then correlated with physical and mental health outcomes across the lifespan.

Findings

The results revealed a graded relationship:

- **Two-thirds of participants** reported at least one adverse childhood experience.
- More than **20% reported three or more**.
- The higher the ACE score, the greater the risk of:
    - Depression, anxiety, and suicide attempts.
    - Substance abuse and risky behaviors.
    - Chronic illnesses such as heart disease, cancer, and diabetes.
    - Shortened life expectancy (up to 20 years in those with the highest ACE scores).

Implications

The ACE study demonstrated that childhood trauma is not a marginal issue but a **determinant of population health**. It reframed trauma as a public health epidemic, linking early adversity to adult outcomes in a systematic, evidence-based way.

Trauma as a Public Health Crisis

The recognition of childhood trauma as widespread and consequential demands a public health approach.

Economic Costs

- Child maltreatment in the United States carries an estimated lifetime economic burden of **over $400 billion annually**, factoring healthcare, productivity losses, criminal justice, and child welfare costs.
- Preventing trauma thus has both humanitarian and economic imperatives.

Intergenerational Transmission

- Childhood trauma increases the risk of difficulties in parenting, perpetuating cycles of adversity.
- Trauma therefore becomes not only an individual but a **societal inheritance**, transmitted across generations unless disrupted by

intervention.

Hidden Epidemic

The term "hidden epidemic" reflects the paradox that childhood trauma is **both ubiquitous and invisible**. Unlike infectious diseases, it spreads silently, often concealed within households, and emerges decades later as chronic illness, psychiatric disorders, and premature death.

Clinical and Policy Implications

1. **Trauma-Informed Care**
    - Schools, clinics, and social services must adopt trauma-informed frameworks.
    - Rather than asking "What's wrong with you?" clinicians must ask, "What happened to you?"
2. **Early Detection**
    - Screening for ACEs in pediatric and primary care settings can identify at-risk children early.
    - Preventive interventions, such as parenting programs and community support, can mitigate long-term effects.
3. **Policy and Advocacy**
    - Addressing poverty, inequality, and systemic violence is essential to reducing childhood trauma.
    - Policymakers must recognize that investments in early childhood safety and stability yield profound long-term returns.

Conclusion

Childhood trauma is not a rare misfortune but a **common developmental challenge** that shapes the health of entire populations. Its invisibility stems from cultural denial, stigma, and systemic neglect, yet the evidence is unequivocal: early adversity has lifelong consequences.

Recognizing childhood trauma as a hidden epidemic compels a shift in perspective. No longer can trauma be viewed as the exception it is the norm. To ignore it is to perpetuate cycles of suffering across generations. To confront it is to open the possibility of prevention, healing, and societal transformation.

In the following chapter, we will explore **how chronic trauma imprints itself on child development**, shaping self-image, worldview, and survival strategies.

CHAPTER TEN: THE IMPRINT OF ABUSE ON CHILD DEVELOPMENT

Introduction

Childhood is a period of rapid neurobiological growth, identity formation, and relational learning. When children are nurtured within safe, predictable environments, they acquire the psychological tools necessary for regulation, exploration, and self-confidence. However, when abuse physical, emotional, or sexual intrudes upon development, the trajectory of growth is profoundly altered.

Unlike acute trauma, childhood abuse often occurs within the relational context where safety should be guaranteed: the family. This paradox fundamentally reshapes a child's sense of self and worldview. Abuse is not simply an event to be remembered; it becomes an **organizing principle of development**, inscribing itself into neural circuits, bodily responses, and internalized beliefs.

This chapter examines:

1. How chronic trauma shapes **self-image and worldview**.
2. The role of **dissociation** as a survival strategy.
3. The developmental consequences of abuse for **identity formation, cognition, and social functioning**.
4. The enduring imprint carried into adolescence and adulthood.

Abuse and the Developing Self

Children construct their sense of self through interactions with caregivers. Praise, attunement, and validation build a sense of worth; neglect, criticism, or violence create an image of the self as defective, unlovable, or dangerous.

Internalization of Blame

- Abused children often conclude, "Something must be wrong with me."
- This self-blame arises because children are cognitively egocentric: they interpret negative events as reflections of their own flaws rather than the failures of caregivers.

Distorted Self-Image

- Abuse fosters pervasive shame.
- The child may feel simultaneously hyper-visible (as a target of ridicule or harm) and invisible (unseen in their pain).
- This duality distorts the child's self-concept, leading to chronic identity confusion.

Worldview of Danger

- If caregivers are unsafe, the world becomes unsafe.
- The child generalizes expectations of betrayal, rejection, or harm to peers, teachers, and later, partners.
- This worldview of perpetual danger underpins hypervigilance, avoidance, and relational difficulties in adulthood.

Dissociation: Survival Strategy in Childhood

One of the most striking imprints of abuse on development is the prevalence of **dissociation**.

Definition

Dissociation is the compartmentalization of experience memories, feelings, or perceptions are disconnected from conscious awareness.

Adaptive Function

- For children who cannot escape abusive environments, dissociation provides psychological escape.
- It allows the child to "go away in the mind" while the body endures harm.
- In this sense, dissociation is protective in the short term.

Developmental Costs

- Chronic dissociation fragments memory, identity, and emotional processing.
- The child grows with gaps in autobiographical narrative and struggles with coherence of self.
- In adulthood, dissociation may manifest as amnesia, depersonalization, derealization, or even dissociative identity disorder.

Cognitive and Emotional Development

Abuse interferes not only with emotional regulation but also with cognitive growth.

Attention and Learning

- Trauma-induced hypervigilance competes with the attentional resources needed for learning.
- The classroom becomes a site of failure, reinforcing feelings of defectiveness.

Emotional Regulation

- Abused children often oscillate between explosive affect and emotional numbing.
- Without models of soothing, they lack the skills for modulating fear, anger, or sadness.

Identity Formation

- Eriksonian theory emphasizes adolescence as a critical period for identity consolidation.
- Abused children enter adolescence burdened with shame and confusion, leading to fragmented or negative identity formation.

Relational Development

Trauma within attachment bonds profoundly affects how children relate to others.

Trust and Intimacy

- If caregivers cannot be trusted, intimacy itself feels dangerous.
- This may lead to avoidance of closeness or compulsive seeking of relationships that replicate abuse.

Peer Relations

- Abused children may be bullied due to low self-esteem or difficulty navigating social cues.
- Alternatively, they may become aggressors, reenacting learned models of power and control.

Intergenerational Transmission

- Without intervention, survivors may struggle in parenting, unintentionally perpetuating patterns of neglect or harshness.

Clinical Vignette

A young girl, repeatedly subjected to emotional humiliation by her mother, learns to dissociate during moments of verbal attack. By adolescence, she struggles with feelings of unreality and gaps in memory. She believes she is fundamentally unworthy of friendship, sabotages relationships out of fear of rejection, and interprets kindness with suspicion. In therapy, her fragmented self-image emerges: one part longs for care, while another anticipates betrayal.

This vignette illustrates how abuse imprints itself not as a single memory but as a **developmental script** governing self-perception and relationships.

Long-Term Consequences

The imprint of childhood abuse reverberates into adulthood across multiple domains:

1. **Psychological Disorders**
    - Complex PTSD, borderline personality disorder, dissociative disorders.
    - High prevalence of depression, anxiety, and substance use.
2. **Physical Health**
    - Elevated risk of autoimmune conditions, gastrointestinal illness, and chronic pain.
    - Stress physiology established in childhood persists, wearing down bodily systems.
3. **Relational Patterns**
    - Cycles of revictimization in intimate relationships.
    - Difficulty parenting, with risk of transmitting trauma to the next generation.

Clinical and Therapeutic Implications

1. **Recognition of Dissociation**
    - Clinicians must be attuned to subtle dissociative phenomena.

    - Misdiagnosis as inattentiveness or defiance risks reinforcing shame.
2. **Restoring Coherence of Self**
    - Therapy should help survivors integrate fragmented self-states into a coherent narrative.
    - This involves both remembering and re-experiencing safety in the therapeutic relationship.
3. **Trauma-Informed Education**
    - Teachers and schools play critical roles in recognizing trauma-related difficulties.
    - Supportive educational environments can buffer against the academic consequences of abuse.

Conclusion

Childhood abuse imprints itself not only in memory but in the very **architecture of development**. It shapes the child's self-image, worldview, emotional regulation, and relational patterns. Dissociation serves as a survival tool, but at the cost of coherence of identity. The result is not merely a wounded child but an altered trajectory of growth, often extending across the lifespan and into future generations.

The next chapter explores how, in the absence of safety, children turn to survival strategies that transform the body itself into a battleground a site of symptoms, defenses, and unspoken memory.

CHAPTER ELEVEN: THE SEARCH FOR SAFETY IN CHILDHOOD

Introduction

For children, safety is not an abstract concept; it is the bedrock of development. Secure environments allow the brain and body to devote resources to exploration, learning, and socialization. Conversely, when safety is absent, survival becomes the dominant imperative.

Abuse, neglect, or inconsistent caregiving deprives children of the secure base necessary for healthy growth. In such circumstances, the body becomes the battleground where trauma is inscribed. Children carry physiological states of alarm, behavioral strategies of hypervigilance or withdrawal, and somatic symptoms that signal unprocessed terror.

This chapter explores:

1. The central role of **caregivers as sources of safety**.
2. The consequences of **absence or betrayal of protection**.
3. How the **body encodes trauma** when safety is lacking.
4. The implications for **development, health, and therapeutic practice**.

Caregivers as Sources of Safety

The concept of **secure attachment** emphasizes that children look to caregivers for co-regulation of distress. When a child is frightened, tired, or hurt, a responsive caregiver provides comfort, enabling the child to return to a state of calm.

The Neurobiology of Safety

- Responsive care giving activates the **parasympathetic nervous system**, lowering cortisol and heart rate.
- Through repeated cycles of stress and soothing, the child learns that distress can be endured and resolved.
- This scaffolds the development of self-regulation.

Safe Haven and Secure Base

- John Bowlby described the caregiver as both a "safe haven" in times of stress and a "secure base" from which to explore.
- When this foundation is present, children develop confidence in both self and others.

The Absence of Protection

When caregivers are absent, inconsistent, or abusive, the very system designed to ensure survival becomes a source of danger.

Attachment Betrayal

- Children depend absolutely on caregivers; betrayal by these figures generates profound confusion.
- The child is biologically driven to seek proximity to the very person who is the source of fear.

Disorganized Attachment

- Research by Mary Main and Judith Solomon identified **disorganized attachment** as characteristic of abused children.
- The child exhibits contradictory behaviors approaching the caregiver for comfort but simultaneously showing fear or freezing.
- This attachment style predicts later difficulties with regulation, dissociation, and interpersonal relationships.

Survival Over Growth

- When safety is absent, the child's nervous system prioritizes **survival over exploration**.
- Cognitive, emotional, and social development are compromised because resources are diverted to vigilance and defense.

The Body as a Battleground

Children without safety carry trauma not only in memory but in their **bodies**.

Somatic Symptoms

- Headaches, stomachaches, and sleep disturbances are common among traumatized children.
- These physical complaints often mask underlying emotional distress, especially when children lack words to describe feelings.

Hyperarousal and Hypoarousal

- Trauma manifests through dysregulated autonomic states:
    - **Hyperarousal**: agitation, startle responses, impulsivity.
    - **Hypoarousal**: numbness, withdrawal, "shutting down."
- The child may alternate between these states depending on environmental triggers.

The Freeze Response

- When neither fight nor flight is possible, children resort to **freeze** a collapse of physical and psychological energy.

- Chronic reliance on freeze states lays groundwork for dissociation and somatic complaints in adulthood.

Clinical Vignette

A boy growing up in a household marked by domestic violence learns that his cries for help will be ignored. Over time, he stops expressing fear and instead develops frequent stomachaches that bring him to the school nurse. His teachers describe him as "quiet but spacey." In therapy years later, he recalls few details of childhood but carries vivid bodily memories: tense muscles, nausea during arguments, and a compulsion to disappear when conflict arises.

This vignette highlights how the **body stores what words cannot express**, becoming both the site and the symptom of trauma.

Developmental Consequences

1. **Neurobiological Imprint**
    - Lack of safety leads to chronic activation of the stress response.
    - Elevated cortisol disrupts hippocampal development, impairing memory and learning.
2. **Behavioral Outcomes**
    - Children may become hyper-compliant in hopes of preventing harm, or oppositional as a defense against vulnerability.
    - Both patterns reflect adaptations to danger, not intrinsic pathology.
3. **Relational Difficulties**
    - Fear of intimacy, mistrust of authority figures, and struggles with peer relationships are common.
    - These difficulties often persist into adolescence and adulthood, complicating education, work, and family life.

The Search for Safety

Despite adversity, children demonstrate remarkable resilience. Their strategies for survival whether dissociation, somatic expression, or hypervigilance are attempts to find safety where none is offered.

Alternative Sources of Safety

- Teachers, mentors, extended family, or peers can serve as protective figures.
- Research shows that even a single stable, supportive adult relationship can buffer against trauma's worst effects.

Therapeutic Safety

- Trauma-focused therapy emphasizes the creation of a **safe therapeutic alliance** before processing memories.
- Without a sense of safety, attempts at disclosure risk retraumatization.

Community and Systems

- Schools, healthcare, and social systems can foster environments where children feel protected.
- Trauma-informed approaches ensure that institutions do not replicate dynamics of powerlessness.

Clinical and Policy Implications

1. **Early Intervention**
    - Pediatricians and educators are uniquely positioned to recognize somatic and behavioral signs of trauma.
    - Early intervention reduces long-term consequences.
2. **Building Safety in Therapy**
    - Interventions such as play therapy, somatic regulation, and relational repair focus on re-establishing a felt sense of safety.
3. **Policy Commitments**
    - Policies that reduce child poverty, prevent domestic violence, and support caregivers directly influence the prevalence of childhood trauma.

Conclusion

The search for safety is central to the lives of traumatized children. When caregivers fail in their protective role, children adapt through strategies that inscribe trauma into their bodies and psyches. These adaptations are not signs of weakness but of survival. Yet, without intervention, they exact heavy costs across development.

Recognizing the centrality of safety reframes both clinical practice and societal responsibility. Safety is not a luxury for children it is a biological necessity. When absent, the body becomes the battleground of trauma. When restored, safety becomes the foundation for healing and growth.

CHAPTER TWELVE: WHAT'S IN A FLASHBACK?

Introduction

Trauma is not remembered in the same way as ordinary experience. Unlike typical autobiographical memories, which are woven into a coherent narrative with a clear temporal and spatial context, traumatic memories often erupt into consciousness as if they were happening in the present moment. These intrusions known as **flashbacks** constitute one of the hallmark symptoms of post-traumatic stress disorder (PTSD) and related conditions.

Flashbacks illustrate the profound way in which trauma alters memory systems. They reflect not a failure to remember but an inability to integrate experience into a safe narrative framework. Survivors do not simply recall trauma; they **relive** it.

This chapter explores:

1. The difference between **sensory memory** and **narrative memory**.
2. Why trauma is **relived, not remembered**.
3. The **neurobiology of flashbacks**, including the roles of the amygdala, hippocampus, and prefrontal cortex.
4. The **subjective experience** of flashbacks and their clinical significance.
5. Implications for treatment and recovery.

Memory Systems and Trauma

To understand flashbacks, it is essential to distinguish between different forms of memory.

Narrative Memory

- Encodes events in a chronological sequence with context, meaning, and language.
- Dependent on hippocampal functioning and prefrontal cortex integration.
- Allows the person to place events in the past and reflect upon them.

Sensory/Implicit Memory

- Encodes fragments of experience sounds, smells, images, bodily sensations.
- Does not require conscious recall; stored primarily in subcortical structures.
- Activated involuntarily in response to triggers.

Trauma disproportionately engages **sensory memory systems** while impairing narrative encoding. As a result, survivors may have vivid sensory fragments without coherent storylines.

Why Trauma Is Relived, Not Remembered

Traumatic experiences overwhelm the nervous system. In states of extreme threat, the **amygdala** (fear center) dominates, while the **hippocampus** (contextual memory) is inhibited by high cortisol levels.

- Ordinary memories are filed as "past."
- Traumatic memories remain unprocessed, with no timestamp, resurfacing as if the danger is present.

This explains why survivors may intellectually "know" they are safe but still feel as if they are back in the moment of trauma when triggered.

The Neurobiology of Flashbacks

The Amygdala

- Hyperactive during trauma and re-experiencing.
- Encodes emotional salience and fear conditioning.
- Reactivated by cues resembling the original trauma (e.g., a smell of smoke after a fire).

The Hippocampus

- Suppressed during trauma, impairing contextual encoding.
- Reduced hippocampal volume is commonly observed in PTSD patients.
- Without hippocampal integration, traumatic fragments remain disconnected.

The Prefrontal Cortex

- Normally regulates emotional responses and provides rational perspective.
- During flashbacks, prefrontal inhibition fails, leaving survivors overwhelmed by sensory fragments.

Together, these dynamics explain why flashbacks feel like involuntary reliving rather than controlled recollection.

Subjective Experience of Flashbacks

Survivors describe flashbacks as sudden intrusions where the body and mind are seized by images, sounds, or sensations.

- **Visual Flashbacks**: vivid, movie-like scenes replayed without control.
- **Somatic Flashbacks**: bodily sensations of pain, pressure, or immobilization.
- **Emotional Flashbacks**: overwhelming waves of fear, shame, or helplessness with no obvious external cause.

Flashbacks often defy language, leaving survivors struggling to explain what has occurred. This inexpressibility contributes to shame, isolation, and avoidance of social contact.

Clinical Vignette

A combat veteran, years after returning from war, hears the sound of fireworks on New Year's Eve. Instantly, his body drops to the ground, heart racing, muscles tense. He sees flashes of light that resemble incoming artillery. He knows he is in his backyard, yet his nervous system insists he is back in the war zone.

This vignette demonstrates how flashbacks collapse time, fusing past and present. The body reacts as though the original threat is renewed.

Flashbacks Across Development

Flashbacks are not uniform across age groups.

- **Children** may not have narrative flashbacks but instead reenact trauma in play, drawings, or behavioral outbursts.
- **Adolescents** may experience emotional flooding, panic, or fragmented imagery.
- **Adults** often present with vivid, intrusive reliving, sometimes triggered by sensory stimuli beyond conscious awareness.

These differences highlight the developmental imprint of trauma on memory systems.

Clinical and Therapeutic Implications

Stabilization Before Processing

- Exposure to traumatic memories must occur only after survivors have developed skills for grounding and regulation.
- Premature exploration risks retraumatization.

Importance of Safety

- Therapeutic settings must provide safety and predictability.
- Grounding techniques (e.g., sensory orientation, breathwork) help anchor survivors in the present.

Narrative Reconstruction

- Effective trauma therapy often involves **transforming sensory fragments into coherent narratives**.
- This process restores the ability to locate trauma in the past rather than reliving it endlessly in the present.

Conclusion

Flashbacks are not signs of weakness but evidence of the profound ways trauma reorganizes memory. Survivors relive, rather than remember, because traumatic experiences bypass narrative systems and remain encoded as sensory fragments. These intrusions testify to the body's insistence on keeping the past alive until integration is achieved.

Understanding flashbacks deepens our grasp of trauma's enduring imprint on the mind and body. In the following chapter, we will examine how trauma not only disrupts memory but **hijacks the brain's capacity for self-regulation**, producing patterns of hyperarousal, triggers, and vigilance that shape daily life.

CHAPTER THIRTEEN: HOW TRAUMA HIJACKS THE BRAIN

Introduction

Trauma does more than create intrusive memories; it fundamentally alters the brain's systems for regulating emotion, attention, and bodily states. Survivors often describe feeling "on edge," unable to relax, and easily triggered by reminders of the past. This state of **hypervigilance and reactivity** reflects changes in the neural circuits that govern self-regulation.

In essence, trauma **hijacks the brain**. Structures designed to keep us safe the amygdala, hippocampus, and prefrontal cortex become dysregulated. The result is a nervous system that misinterprets benign signals as threats, activating fight, flight, or freeze responses when no danger is present.

This chapter examines:

1. The **neurobiological breakdown of self-regulation**.
2. How **triggers and reactivity** emerge.
3. The role of **hypervigilance** as a survival adaptation.
4. The subjective and clinical manifestations of a hijacked brain.
5. Implications for therapy and recovery.

Self-Regulation and Its Breakdown

The Function of Self-Regulation

In a healthy nervous system, the brain balances arousal and calm, enabling flexible responses to challenges. Self-regulation involves:

- **Emotional regulation**: calming oneself after distress.
- **Attention control**: shifting focus away from intrusive thoughts.
- **Physiological regulation**: maintaining stable heart rate, breath, and cortisol levels.

Trauma's Impact

- Repeated trauma destabilizes these systems.
- Survivors often oscillate between **hyperarousal** (panic, rage,

agitation) and **hypoarousal** (numbness, shutdown).

- This instability reflects chronic dysregulation of the autonomic nervous system.

The Neurobiology of Hijacking

Amygdala Hyperactivation

- The amygdala becomes hypersensitive after trauma.
- Even subtle cues (tone of voice, sudden noise) can trigger alarm responses.
- This accounts for exaggerated startle responses in PTSD.

Hippocampal Impairment

- Trauma disrupts contextual memory, preventing survivors from distinguishing past from present.
- Reduced hippocampal volume has been consistently observed in trauma survivors.
- Without proper context, harmless cues are linked to danger.

Prefrontal Cortex Underactivation

- Normally, the prefrontal cortex exerts "top-down" control over the amygdala.
- In trauma survivors, this regulation weakens, allowing emotional responses to override rational thought.
- This explains why survivors often say, *"I know I'm safe, but I don't feel safe."*

Triggers and Reactivity

The Nature of Triggers

- Triggers are stimuli often sensory that resemble aspects of trauma.
- They need not be logical: the smell of cologne, the slamming of a door, or even a season of the year can reactivate trauma.

Physiological Reactivity

- Triggers activate the sympathetic nervous system, causing racing heart, sweating, muscle tension.
- Survivors often describe feeling as if they are "back in it," despite knowing intellectually they are not.

The Unpredictability of Triggers

- Because many triggers are unconscious, survivors may feel blindsided by sudden panic or dissociation.
- This unpredictability contributes to avoidance behaviors, as individuals try to minimize exposure to possible reminders.

Hypervigilance as Adaptation

Hypervigilance is often misunderstood as paranoia or anxiety. In reality, it is an adaptive response to repeated danger.

- **Definition**: persistent scanning of the environment for threats.
- **Function**: increases likelihood of detecting danger early.
- **Cost**: prevents rest, impairs concentration, and contributes to exhaustion.

From an evolutionary standpoint, hypervigilance increases survival odds in unsafe environments. However, when carried into safe contexts, it becomes maladaptive, disrupting daily life.

Clinical Vignette

A woman who survived childhood abuse describes always sitting with her back to the wall in restaurants, scanning for exits, and jumping at the sound of footsteps behind her. She cannot watch television without hyperanalyzing background noises. While these strategies once helped her survive, they now prevent her from experiencing relaxation or connection.

This vignette illustrates how trauma hijacks perception, trapping survivors in a constant state of readiness for danger.

The Subjective Experience of a Hijacked Brain

Survivors commonly report:

- Feeling "hijacked" by emotions they cannot control.

- Sudden shifts into rage, terror, or despair.
- Chronic tension and difficulty sleeping.
- A sense of being at the mercy of their own nervous systems.

These experiences reinforce shame and self-blame, as survivors may believe they are "crazy" or weak. In reality, these are predictable consequences of altered neurobiology.

Clinical and Therapeutic Implications

Grounding and Regulation Skills

- Before processing trauma, survivors must learn to regulate arousal.
- Techniques include breathwork, mindfulness, and sensory grounding.

Psychoeducation

- Understanding that symptoms are biologically based reduces shame.
- Survivors often find relief in learning that hypervigilance and reactivity are adaptive responses, not personal failures.

Rewiring Through Therapy

- Approaches such as EMDR, neurofeedback, and somatic therapies aim to restore balance to the brain's regulation systems.
- Relational therapies emphasize co-regulation, teaching survivors to feel safe in the presence of others.

Conclusion

Trauma hijacks the brain by sensitizing fear circuits, impairing contextual memory, and weakening regulatory systems. Survivors live with nervous systems that misinterpret safety as danger, producing cycles of reactivity, triggers, and hypervigilance.

Understanding this hijacking reframes trauma not as a problem of willpower but as a neurobiological adaptation gone awry. Treatment, therefore, must focus not only on memory but also on **restoring regulation and safety** at the most fundamental brain and body levels.

In the next chapter, we will explore **the unspoken legacy of trauma shame, secrecy, and silence and how these social dimensions deepen isolation for survivors.**

CHAPTER FOURTEEN: THE UNSPOKEN LEGACY OF TRAUMA

Introduction

While the neurobiology of trauma reveals how the brain and body are altered by overwhelming experiences, the **social dimensions of trauma** carry equally profound consequences. Survivors frequently live not only with flashbacks, triggers, and hypervigilance, but also with **shame, secrecy, and silence**. These elements, though less visible than physiological changes, shape the trajectory of trauma recovery and often determine whether survivors find healing or remain trapped in isolation.

Trauma is rarely endured alone; it unfolds within families, communities, and societies. Yet cultural and interpersonal responses frequently discourage disclosure. Survivors may be silenced by disbelief, stigma, or fear of reprisal. This chapter explores:

1. **Shame as a core legacy of trauma**.
2. **Secrecy and concealment** as survival strategies.
3. The role of **silence and societal denial**.
4. How these dynamics perpetuate isolation.
5. Pathways to breaking silence and restoring connection.

Shame: The Hidden Wound

The Nature of Shame

Shame differs from guilt. Guilt says, *"I did something bad."* Shame says, *"I am bad."* For trauma survivors, especially those who endured abuse, the violation often becomes internalized as self-defectiveness.

Mechanisms of Shame

- **Perpetrator messages**: abusers frequently blame victims, instilling the belief that they caused their own suffering.
- **Physiological overwhelm**: the loss of control during trauma reinforces feelings of helplessness and worthlessness.
- **Cultural stigma**: survivors of sexual violence, domestic abuse, or war atrocities are often treated as tainted rather than harmed.

Clinical Observations

Shame manifests as avoidance of eye contact, difficulty seeking help, and self-silencing in therapy. Survivors may struggle to articulate their experiences, fearing judgment or rejection.

Secrecy as Survival

Protective Silence

Many survivors learn to conceal trauma as a way of navigating dangerous environments. Children in abusive households, for example, may keep secrets to avoid retaliation or preserve family stability.

Long-Term Consequences

What begins as a survival strategy becomes corrosive over time:

- Secrets isolate survivors from supportive relationships.
- Energy is consumed by maintaining concealment.
- Secrecy reinforces the belief that trauma is unspeakable.

Clinical Vignette

A man abused by a trusted mentor never disclosed his experiences for decades. Outwardly successful, he carried an internal narrative of shame. Only in midlife therapy did he reveal his secret, describing the silence as "a prison built inside myself."

Silence and Societal Denial

Cultural Factors

Societies often collude in silencing trauma:

- **War veterans** may be discouraged from discussing atrocities, lest they disrupt patriotic narratives.
- **Survivors of sexual violence** may face victim-blaming.
- **Children of abuse** are often met with disbelief, especially when perpetrators are respected figures.

Institutional Betrayal

When schools, religious institutions, or governments fail to acknowledge abuse, survivors experience "institutional betrayal." This compounds trauma, as trusted systems become sources of harm rather than support.

The Weight of Silence

Collective denial prevents recognition, perpetuates stigma, and hinders prevention. Without acknowledgment, survivors remain burdened by what society refuses to see.

The Isolation of Survivors

The interplay of shame, secrecy, and silence isolates survivors in profound ways.

- **Interpersonal Isolation**: Survivors may withdraw from relationships, fearing disclosure will lead to rejection.
- **Emotional Isolation**: Unspoken trauma fragments self-experience, leaving survivors disconnected from their own emotions.
- **Societal Isolation**: Stigma and denial create barriers to seeking professional or communal support.

This isolation deepens suffering, as trauma thrives in environments of disconnection.

Breaking Silence: Toward Healing

Testimony and Bearing Witness

Healing often begins when survivors speak and are heard. Testimony transforms isolated experiences into shared narratives, affirming that the burden belongs not solely to the survivor but to the broader human community.

The Role of Safe Relationships

Therapeutic alliances, support groups, and trusted friendships provide contexts in which survivors can risk disclosure. Safety is the precondition for breaking silence.

Collective Movements

- The women's movement in the 1970s exposed the prevalence of domestic violence and sexual assault.
- Veteran advocacy brought recognition of combat trauma.
- Recent social movements (#MeToo, child abuse inquiries) illustrate the power of collective voice in dismantling secrecy.

Clinical Implications

Therapists must recognize that disclosure is not simply recounting facts; it is an act of courage that risks disrupting entrenched dynamics of shame and secrecy. Sensitive listening, validation, and containment are essential.

Conclusion

The unspoken legacy of trauma extends beyond neurobiology into the realms of shame, secrecy, and silence. These forces magnify suffering by isolating survivors and perpetuating stigma. Yet they are not immutable. Through testimony, safe relationships, and collective acknowledgment, survivors can transform silence into speech and reclaim belonging.

CHAPTER FIFTEEN: THE LIMITS OF TALK THERAPY

Introduction

For much of the 20th century, **psychological healing was equated with talking.** The dominant paradigm psychoanalysis rested on the belief that insight derived from verbal expression could alleviate symptoms. Later, cognitive-behavioral therapy (CBT) advanced a structured model for identifying maladaptive thoughts and reshaping behaviors through dialogue. Both approaches presumed that words could adequately access and transform traumatic memory.

However, the clinical reality of trauma has consistently challenged this assumption. Survivors often describe therapy as helpful for understanding, but insufficient for altering the visceral grip of trauma on body and brain. Many report, *"I know it wasn't my fault, but I still feel like it was,"* or *"Talking helps in the office, but my body still panics when I'm triggered."* These discrepancies reveal the **limits of language-centered therapies** when confronted with trauma's imprint.

This chapter explores:

1. The historical reliance on talk-based therapies.
2. Why words alone often fail trauma survivors.
3. Case examples where psychoanalysis and CBT were insufficient.
4. The importance of body-based and experiential modalities as complements.

The Origins of Talk Therapy

Psychoanalysis and the Talking Cure

Sigmund Freud's early work, inspired by Josef Breuer's treatment of "hysteria," proposed that repressed traumatic experiences caused neurotic symptoms. Through free association, patients could give voice to hidden memories, releasing pent-up affect. This idea **"the talking cure"** dominated early psychotherapy.

Cognitive-Behavioral Therapy (CBT)

By the 1970s, CBT emerged as the most empirically validated form of therapy. CBT focused on restructuring distorted cognitions and modifying maladaptive behaviors. Its structured protocols made it attractive for clinical trials, especially in PTSD research among veterans.

Both traditions elevated language as the central tool for recovery.

Why Words Fail Trauma Survivors

Implicit vs. Explicit Memory

Trauma is not encoded in the same way as ordinary memory.

- **Explicit memory** (narrative, verbal) is accessible to conscious recall.
- **Implicit memory** (sensory, emotional, bodily) operates below awareness.

Trauma is stored largely in implicit systems. Survivors may not have coherent narratives to tell, rendering traditional talk therapy insufficient.

Neurobiological Barriers

- **Hippocampal dysfunction** prevents coherent sequencing of traumatic events.
- **Amygdala hyperactivation** floods survivors with emotion, impairing verbal expression.
- **Prefrontal underactivation** reduces capacity for reflective narrative.

Thus, asking survivors to "talk it through" may overwhelm rather than heal.

Dissociation and Speechlessness

Many trauma survivors experience **speechless terror** a state in which language shuts down under threat. When trauma memories are reactivated in therapy, survivors may freeze, dissociate, or lose access to words entirely.

Case Examples: When Talking Is Not Enough

Case 1: Psychoanalysis and Combat Trauma

A Vietnam veteran spent years in analytic therapy, revisiting childhood experiences and dreams. Although he developed insight into his personality, his flashbacks persisted. He stated, *"I could talk about my father endlessly, but the war still lived in my body."*

Case 2: CBT and Childhood Abuse

A woman who endured chronic childhood sexual abuse engaged in trauma-focused CBT. She successfully identified "distorted cognitions" (e.g., "It was my fault"). Yet despite cognitive shifts, she continued to experience panic attacks when touched unexpectedly.

These cases highlight the gap between **cognitive understanding** and **embodied regulation**.

The Pitfalls of Verbal-Centric Approaches

1. **Overemphasis on Rationality**: Trauma is not fundamentally irrational but subcortical; logic alone cannot regulate dysregulated nervous systems.
2. **Risk of Retraumatization**: Forcing premature verbal disclosure may overwhelm survivors, reinforcing helplessness.
3. **Neglect of the Body**: Talk therapies often ignore somatic manifestations tension, hyperarousal, dissociation.
4. **Cultural Limitations**: Many cultures prioritize storytelling, ritual, or collective practices over private verbal analysis.

The Place of Talk Therapy in Recovery

This critique does not dismiss the value of talk therapy. Language provides:

- **Validation**: naming experiences reduces isolation.
- **Meaning-making**: constructing narratives helps integrate fragmented memories.
- **Cognitive reframing**: challenging distorted beliefs can reduce shame.

However, talk therapy must be situated as one **piece of a broader therapeutic landscape**, not the sole or primary route to healing.

Emerging Alternatives

Because words alone often fail, clinicians have increasingly turned toward **integrative approaches**:

- **Eye Movement Desensitization and Reprocessing (EMDR)**: engages bilateral stimulation to process traumatic memories.
- **Somatic Experiencing and yoga**: emphasize regulation through the body.
- **Neurofeedback**: retrains brainwave patterns.
- **Theater and expressive arts**: provide non-verbal modes of processing.

These modalities recognize that trauma resides as much in the body and brain circuits as in language.

Conclusion

Talk therapy has played a foundational role in mental health treatment, but trauma reveals its limits. Survivors often carry wounds that resist verbal processing, manifesting instead in dysregulated physiology, fragmented memory, and embodied terror. While words can validate and reframe, they rarely suffice to restore regulation and safety.

As the field has evolved, recognition of these limits has paved the way for innovative treatments that go beyond language, engaging the body, brain, and relational systems. In the next chapter, we will examine **Eye Movement Desensitization and Reprocessing (EMDR)**, a pioneering method that attempts to bridge verbal and non-verbal domains in trauma recovery.

CHAPTER SIXTEEN: EMDR (EYE MOVEMENT DESENSITIZATION AND REPROCESSING)

Introduction

Few therapeutic innovations have sparked as much debate in the trauma field as **Eye Movement Desensitization and Reprocessing (EMDR)**. Introduced in the late 1980s by psychologist Francine Shapiro, EMDR began as a seemingly unconventional technique: asking clients to recall distressing memories while simultaneously engaging in **bilateral stimulation** usually through guided eye movements.

What appeared at first glance as an odd or gimmicky intervention gradually gained empirical support, particularly for post-traumatic stress disorder (PTSD). Today, EMDR is recognized by organizations such as the **World Health Organization (WHO)**, the **American Psychiatric Association (APA)**, and the **Department of Veterans Affairs (VA)** as an effective treatment for trauma.

This chapter examines:

1. The origins and theoretical foundations of EMDR.
2. Its proposed mechanisms of action.
3. Evidence from clinical trials and case studies.
4. Ongoing debates and controversies.
5. The place of EMDR within the broader landscape of trauma recovery.

Origins of EMDR

Francine Shapiro's Discovery

In 1987, Francine Shapiro noticed that her own distressing thoughts seemed to diminish when her eyes moved back and forth rapidly. Intrigued, she experimented with guiding clients through similar movements while recalling traumatic memories. The results were striking memories lost their intensity, and distress lessened.

Shapiro formalized this into a structured eight-phase protocol, which she termed **Eye Movement Desensitization (later "and Reprocessing") Therapy**.

Initial Skepticism

The therapy was met with skepticism, partly due to its unusual origins and apparent simplicity. Critics derided it as pseudoscience or a placebo effect. Yet as clinical trials accumulated, evidence increasingly suggested EMDR produced significant improvements for PTSD.

The EMDR Protocol

The EMDR process follows an **eight-phase structure**:

1. **History-taking and treatment planning**: gathering background and identifying target memories.
2. **Preparation**: teaching grounding and stabilization techniques.
3. **Assessment**: identifying a specific traumatic image, negative belief, desired positive belief, and current distress level.
4. **Desensitization**: recalling the memory while engaging in bilateral stimulation (eye movements, taps, or tones).
5. **Installation**: strengthening the positive belief while continuing bilateral stimulation.
6. **Body scan**: noticing residual tension or discomfort.
7. **Closure**: ensuring stability before ending the session.
8. **Re-evaluation**: assessing progress in subsequent sessions.

The method is distinctive in its emphasis on both **re-experiencing traumatic material** and simultaneously engaging in **dual-attention stimulation**.

Mechanisms of Action

The precise mechanisms underlying EMDR remain debated. Several hypotheses exist:

1. **Working Memory Taxation Hypothesis**
    - Holding a traumatic memory in mind while performing eye movements taxes working memory capacity.
    - This reduces the vividness and emotional intensity of the memory.
2. **REM Sleep Analogy**
    - Bilateral eye movements resemble the rapid eye movement phase of sleep, during which emotional memories are consolidated.
    - EMDR may mimic or facilitate similar processing pathways.

1. **Neurobiological Regulation**
   - Imaging studies suggest EMDR reduces activation in the amygdala and increases prefrontal control.
   - Bilateral stimulation may enhance inter-hemispheric communication, supporting integration of fragmented memory traces.

Though no single mechanism has been definitively proven, research indicates that EMDR uniquely combines **exposure, cognitive restructuring, and neurological regulation.**

Evidence of Effectiveness

Randomized Controlled Trials (RCTs)

- Multiple RCTs demonstrate that EMDR is as effective as trauma-focused CBT in reducing PTSD symptoms.
- Some studies suggest EMDR works more rapidly, with fewer sessions required.

Meta-Analyses

- Meta-analyses consistently confirm EMDR's efficacy for PTSD across diverse populations, including veterans, sexual assault survivors, and disaster victims.

Beyond PTSD

Emerging evidence suggests EMDR may help with:

- **Complex trauma** (though results are more variable).
- **Phobias and anxiety disorders.**
- **Depression linked to trauma histories.**

Clinical Vignettes

- **Combat Veteran**: A soldier haunted by a roadside bombing reported that after several EMDR sessions, the memory no longer triggered panic; instead, it became "just something that happened."

- **Childhood Abuse Survivor**: A woman with chronic flashbacks found EMDR allowed her to reframe the abuse as the responsibility of the perpetrator rather than her own fault.

These cases illustrate how EMDR helps recontextualize traumatic memory, reducing its emotional charge.

Controversies and Critiques

Despite its recognition, EMDR remains controversial:

1. **The Role of Eye Movements**
    - Some argue that eye movements are unnecessary, and that EMDR works primarily as a form of exposure therapy.
    - Others contend bilateral stimulation provides unique benefits.
2. **Rapid Gains vs. Depth of Healing**
    - Critics question whether EMDR produces lasting integration or merely symptom reduction.
    - Some survivors report profound change; others describe only temporary relief.
3. **Accessibility and Training**
    - EMDR requires specialized training, limiting availability.
    - Poorly trained practitioners may misuse the method, risking retraumatization.
4. **Cultural Reception**
    - EMDR's mechanistic appearance sometimes clashes with cultural traditions that favor relational or ritual-based healing.

EMDR in the Broader Context

While EMDR is not a panacea, it has earned a secure place in trauma treatment. Its strengths include:

- Efficiency in reducing distress.
- Empirical validation across populations.

- Accessibility for clients who struggle with verbal disclosure.

Yet EMDR works best when integrated with broader therapeutic strategies, including stabilization, relational support, and somatic regulation.

Conclusion

EMDR represents a pivotal development in the evolution of trauma treatment. By combining exposure to traumatic memory with bilateral stimulation, it bridges the gap between cognitive and somatic approaches. Although questions remain regarding its mechanisms and limitations, EMDR has helped millions of survivors reduce the grip of trauma.

Its success underscores a central theme of modern trauma research: **healing requires more than words.** In the next chapter, we turn to another frontier **neurofeedback**, which aims to retrain the traumatized brain through direct regulation of neural activity.

CHAPTER SEVENTEEN: NEUROFEEDBACK AND REWIRING THE BRAIN

Introduction

Trauma alters not only memory but also the very rhythms of the brain. Survivors often describe feeling hijacked by intrusive states of hyperarousal, dissociation, or emotional numbing conditions that traditional psychotherapy cannot always reach. Advances in neuroscience have revealed that trauma rewires stress circuits, creating patterns of dysregulation that persist long after the threat has passed.

Neurofeedback, also known as electroencephalographic (EEG) biofeedback, offers a novel approach: training individuals to regulate their own brain activity by providing real-time feedback on neural oscillations. Rather than relying solely on language or cognitive strategies, neurofeedback engages the brain at its physiological roots. For many trauma survivors, this represents a transformative pathway one in which the nervous system itself learns new patterns of stability and resilience.

This chapter explores:

1. The scientific foundations of neurofeedback.
2. Its historical development and entry into trauma treatment.
3. Mechanisms of action in rewiring neural circuits.
4. Evidence of effectiveness in PTSD and developmental trauma.
5. Case studies illustrating clinical application.
6. Limitations, challenges, and future directions.

The Science of Neurofeedback

Brain Rhythms and Dysregulation

The human brain produces oscillatory patterns commonly categorized as delta, theta, alpha, beta, and gamma waves. Each frequency band corresponds to distinct states of consciousness, from deep sleep (delta) to focused attention (beta) and integrative processing (gamma).

Trauma disrupts these rhythms:

- **Hyperarousal** often manifests as excess high-beta activity.
- **Dissociation and numbing** may be reflected in abnormal theta or alpha patterns.
- **Fragmented attention** corresponds with unstable oscillatory transitions.

By measuring and displaying these rhythms in real time, neurofeedback allows individuals to **see and modulate their own brain states.**

Feedback Loops and Learning

In neurofeedback sessions, electrodes measure EEG activity, which is translated into visual or auditory signals such as a video game responding to the client's brainwaves. When the brain shifts toward desired patterns, the game progresses; when it moves toward dysregulation, feedback signals pause. Over time, the brain learns to self-regulate through **operant conditioning**.

Historical Development

Neurofeedback emerged in the 1960s through the work of researchers such as **Joe Kamiya** and **Barry Sterman**, who demonstrated that individuals could learn to voluntarily control brainwave activity. Early applications focused on epilepsy and attention-deficit disorders.

Its application to trauma came later, as clinicians noticed parallels between trauma-related dysregulation and other neurological conditions. By the late 1990s and early 2000s, pioneers such as **Bessel van der Kolk** began integrating neurofeedback into trauma therapy, reporting significant improvements in self-regulation and affect stability among survivors.

Mechanisms of Action

The precise ways in which neurofeedback facilitates healing remain under investigation, but several mechanisms are hypothesized:

1. **Restoring Autonomic Balance**
    - By stabilizing oscillatory activity, neurofeedback reduces sympathetic overactivation and strengthens parasympathetic recovery.
2. **Enhancing Prefrontal Control**
    - Training supports connectivity between the prefrontal cortex and limbic structures, improving emotional regulation.

3. **Interrupting Trauma Loops**
    - Survivors often cycle between hypervigilance and dissociation. Neurofeedback helps establish more flexible, adaptive state transitions.
4. **Neuroplasticity**
    - Repeated training induces long-term changes in neural networks, fostering resilience.

Evidence of Effectiveness

PTSD and Complex Trauma

Several clinical trials demonstrate significant reductions in PTSD symptoms following neurofeedback:

- Improvements in sleep, attention, and emotional regulation.
- Reductions in flashbacks, nightmares, and startle responses.
- Enhanced capacity for interpersonal connection.

Developmental Trauma

Children with histories of neglect and abuse often show dramatic gains:

- Increased ability to focus in school.
- Decreased impulsivity and aggression.
- Enhanced capacity to form trusting relationships.

Comparative Outcomes

Studies suggest neurofeedback is particularly effective when combined with other modalities, such as talk therapy or EMDR. Rather than replacing psychotherapy, it provides a **physiological foundation** upon which narrative integration can occur.

Clinical Vignettes

- **Veteran with Chronic PTSD**: After years of medication and talk therapy, a veteran still suffered from severe insomnia and hypervigilance. Following 40 sessions of neurofeedback, he reported sleeping through the night for the first time in decades and felt "present" with his family again.

- **Child with Attachment Trauma**: A 9-year-old foster child, prone to rage and dissociation, underwent neurofeedback training. Over six months, her emotional outbursts decreased, and teachers noted her increased engagement in learning.

These cases illustrate how direct regulation of neural activity can restore capacities that talk-based interventions often cannot reach.

Limitations and Challenges

Despite its promise, neurofeedback faces several obstacles:

1. **Access and Cost**: Sessions require specialized equipment and multiple appointments, making them expensive and less accessible.
2. **Standardization Issues**: Protocols vary widely, and not all practitioners are equally trained.
3. **Research Gaps**: While evidence is growing, large-scale randomized controlled trials remain limited.
4. **Integration with Therapy**: Neurofeedback is not a stand-alone cure; without relational and narrative integration, some gains may be temporary.

Future Directions

Advances in **real-time fMRI neurofeedback** and **closed-loop systems** promise more precise targeting of dysregulated networks. Integration with wearable technologies could make neurofeedback more accessible outside clinical settings. As the neuroscience of trauma evolves, neurofeedback may become a standard tool for enhancing resilience and recovery.

Conclusion

Neurofeedback represents a radical shift in trauma treatment: rather than relying on words or memory processing alone, it teaches the brain to **self-regulate from within.** For survivors whose nervous systems remain trapped in cycles of fear, dissociation, or emotional chaos, neurofeedback offers hope for stability and reconnection.

Yet it is not a silver bullet. True healing requires integration of body, brain, and relationship. Neurofeedback provides the neural foundation, but recovery unfolds fully when combined with community, therapy, and meaning-making.

In the following chapter, we will explore how **community and connection** play a central role in trauma healing reminding us that while the brain may be trained individually, recovery ultimately occurs in relationship with others.

CHAPTER EIGHTEEN: THE HEALING POWER OF COMMUNITY & CONNECTION

Introduction

Trauma is often defined as an event that overwhelms the nervous system, but its deepest wounds are social. Survivors frequently report feelings of **isolation, shame, and alienation** as though their suffering cuts them off from others. Trauma convinces the individual that they are fundamentally different, damaged, or unworthy of love.

Healing, therefore, is not only a matter of rewiring the brain or resolving traumatic memories. It requires **restoring the capacity for connection.** Community, relationships, and shared meaning provide the context in which recovery can take root. This chapter explores:

1. The social impact of trauma and why isolation intensifies suffering.
2. The role of group therapy and peer support.
3. The protective power of belonging and social bonds.
4. Cross-cultural perspectives on community healing.
5. The risks of retraumatization within communities.
6. Implications for trauma-informed systems and societies.

The Social Wounds of Trauma

Isolation and Alienation

Survivors often describe feeling as though they live "outside" normal life. They may withdraw from family and friends, avoid intimacy, or struggle to trust others. This alienation is not merely psychological but rooted in neurobiology:

- The **ventral vagal system**, which governs social engagement, often shuts down in trauma survivors.
- Hypervigilance makes interpersonal contact threatening rather than soothing.
- Shame convinces survivors that their suffering is unspeakable.

The Role of Stigma

Cultural stigma surrounding mental illness, PTSD, or abuse deepens isolation. Veterans may feel misunderstood by civilians; survivors of sexual violence may fear disbelief or blame; children may internalize abuse as a personal defect.

Community as Antidote

Group Therapy and Peer Support

Group therapy provides a space where survivors realize they are not alone. Hearing others articulate similar struggles validates their experiences and reduces shame. Peer support programs such as veteran groups, survivor networks, and recovery circles reinforce the healing power of shared narratives.

- **Normalization**: "What I feel is not madness; it is a common response to trauma."
- **Mutual aid**: Members provide empathy, encouragement, and accountability.
- **Resilience building**: Sharing stories of survival fosters collective strength.

Belonging as Regulation

Research confirms that **social connection regulates the nervous system.** Safe relationships calm the amygdala, stabilize cortisol levels, and restore vagal tone. In essence, human connection is a form of biological regulation, counteracting the hyperarousal of trauma.

The Healing Power of Social Bonds

Attachment Repair

Trauma often disrupts attachment, especially when abuse or neglect occurs in childhood. Healing involves re-establishing bonds of trust and safety. Therapists, mentors, or supportive partners can serve as **corrective attachment figures**, demonstrating that intimacy can coexist with safety.

Ritual and Collective Healing

Across cultures, healing rituals emphasize community:

- Indigenous ceremonies often involve communal storytelling, drumming, or dancing.
- Holocaust survivors described the importance of gathering with fellow survivors to bear witness.
- In post-conflict societies, truth and reconciliation processes attempt to restore social fabric.

These examples illustrate that trauma is not only an individual wound but a collective one, requiring **communal acknowledgment and repair.**

Risks and Challenges

Not all communities are safe. Survivors may face retraumatization if their disclosures are met with disbelief, minimization, or blame. Additionally:

- **Toxic group dynamics** can replicate abuse patterns.
- **Codependency** may emerge in peer groups.
- Survivors may feel pressured to remain silent to preserve group cohesion.

Thus, the presence of skilled facilitators and trauma-informed structures is essential.

Trauma-Informed Systems

Healing through community is not limited to therapy groups; it requires **trauma-informed institutions**. Schools, healthcare, workplaces, and justice systems must recognize the role of trauma and avoid practices that exacerbate harm.

Key principles include:

1. **Safety** – creating predictable, non-threatening environments.
2. **Trustworthiness** – consistency and transparency in relationships.
3. **Collaboration** – involving survivors in shaping their care.
4. **Empowerment** – reinforcing choice and autonomy.
5. **Cultural sensitivity** – acknowledging diverse traditions of healing.

When entire systems adopt trauma-informed approaches, survivors find not just isolated pockets of support but a society more capable of fostering recovery.

Case Studies

- **Veteran Peer Network**: A group of Iraq War veterans reported that talking with each other succeeded where therapy had failed, because only peers could understand the moral injuries of combat.
- **Domestic Violence Survivors**: Women in a shelter found strength through nightly storytelling circles, reclaiming their voices and recognizing shared resilience.
- **School-Based Trauma Program**: A middle school that implemented trauma-informed practices saw dramatic reductions in disciplinary incidents, demonstrating the ripple effects of community healing.

Conclusion

Trauma divides, isolates, and silences. Community restores, connects, and gives voice. While therapies such as EMDR and neurofeedback address the neurological imprints of trauma, **healing cannot be sustained without social reconnection.** Survivors need safe spaces where they are seen, believed, and valued.

The science is clear: belonging is not optional it is a biological necessity. The path forward requires weaving trauma-informed communities, where healing is not a private burden but a collective responsibility.

In the next chapter, we will explore how survivors can **reconnect with their bodies** through movement and creativity examining the role of yoga, theater, and somatic therapies in reclaiming agency and vitality.

CHAPTER NINETEEN: YOGA, THEATER, AND SOMATIC THERAPIES

Introduction

Trauma is stored not only in memory but in the body. Survivors often describe feeling tense, numb, or disconnected from their physical selves. They may live with chronic pain, shallow breathing, or sudden bodily reactions that seem inexplicable. Traditional psychotherapy can provide insight into these experiences, yet many survivors report that words alone are insufficient to restore a sense of wholeness.

This recognition has given rise to **somatic therapies** approaches that target the body directly through movement, awareness, and creativity. Among these, yoga, theater, and other expressive practices have emerged as powerful tools for restoring safety, reclaiming agency, and fostering integration. This chapter examines:

1. Why trauma is a bodily as well as psychological condition.
2. Yoga as a method for calming the nervous system and restoring embodiment.
3. Theater and roleplay as pathways to reclaim voice and agency.
4. The broader field of somatic therapies, including dance, martial arts, and breathwork.
5. Clinical evidence and case studies.
6. Challenges and cautions in somatic work.

Trauma as a Bodily Imprint

Neuroscientific studies demonstrate that traumatic stress alters body awareness and physiological regulation. Survivors often experience:

- **Hyperarousal**: rapid heartbeat, shallow breathing, muscle tension.
- **Hypoarousal**: numbness, dissociation, feeling "frozen" or disconnected.
- **Somatic flashbacks**: body sensations linked to trauma without conscious memory.

The body becomes a battleground constantly signaling threat, even in safe environments. Somatic therapies aim to **restore a sense of ownership and safety in the body**, teaching survivors to notice, tolerate, and gradually integrate physical sensations.

Yoga and Trauma Healing

The Physiology of Yoga

Yoga combines movement, breathing, and mindfulness all of which directly regulate the autonomic nervous system. Practices such as slow breathing increase vagal tone, calming the amygdala and reducing cortisol. Gentle postures cultivate interoception the ability to sense what is happening inside the body.

Trauma-Sensitive Yoga

Standard yoga classes can sometimes be overwhelming for trauma survivors, especially if instructors use physical touch or emphasize performance. **Trauma-sensitive yoga (TSY)**, pioneered by David Emerson and colleagues, modifies the practice by emphasizing:

- Choice and empowerment rather than compliance.
- Non-coercive language ("you might try..." instead of "do this").
- Attention to grounding, breathing, and safe movement.

Clinical trials suggest that TSY can reduce PTSD symptoms, enhance emotional regulation, and foster a renewed sense of embodiment.

Case Example

A woman with a history of childhood sexual abuse described years of feeling estranged from her own body. Through trauma-sensitive yoga, she gradually learned to tolerate sensations of breath and movement without fear. She reported: "For the first time, I feel like my body belongs to me."

Theater and Roleplay

Reclaiming Voice and Agency

Trauma often silences survivors, robbing them of language or distorting their self-narratives. Theater offers a space to experiment with new roles, reclaim voice, and reimagine identity. Through enactment, survivors can express emotions that words alone cannot capture.

Psychodrama and Playback Theater

- **Psychodrama** involves structured roleplay in which participants act out scenes from their lives, experimenting with new outcomes.
- **Playback theater** invites participants to tell personal stories, which are then enacted by a group of performers creating communal recognition and validation.

Both forms emphasize **agency, creativity, and social witnessing**, counteracting the passivity and isolation of trauma.

Case Example

In a therapeutic theater group for survivors of domestic violence, participants reported that roleplay helped them confront feelings of fear and anger while discovering inner strength. One woman reflected: "On stage, I spoke words I could never say at home. Now I know my voice has power."

Other Somatic Pathways

Beyond yoga and theater, a variety of body-based practices show promise in trauma healing:

- **Dance therapy**: Facilitates expression of emotions through movement.
- **Martial arts**: Practices like aikido or tai chi foster discipline, grounding, and self-confidence.
- **Breathwork**: Techniques such as coherent breathing stabilize the autonomic nervous system.

- **Somatic experiencing (Peter Levine)**: Focuses on gently releasing trapped survival responses in the body.

Each of these methods emphasizes **agency, safety, and integration** key principles for survivors.

Clinical Evidence

Emerging research supports somatic therapies as complementary interventions for trauma:

- Studies of trauma-sensitive yoga report significant reductions in PTSD symptoms.
- Dance and movement therapies are linked to improved mood, social connectedness, and body image.
- Somatic experiencing shows promise in reducing physiological markers of stress.

While evidence is still developing, findings suggest that **body-based therapies enhance outcomes when combined with psychotherapy and community support.**

Challenges and Cautions

Somatic work is not without risks. Survivors may feel overwhelmed by body sensations or triggered by certain movements. To prevent retraumatization:

- Therapists must pace interventions carefully.
- Choice and consent should be emphasized at every step.
- Somatic work is most effective when integrated into a broader therapeutic plan.

Conclusion

Yoga, theater, and somatic therapies highlight a central truth: trauma is not just an event in memory but an ongoing condition in the body. By reconnecting with breath, movement, and creativity, survivors reclaim agency, presence, and vitality.

These approaches demonstrate that healing is not solely about remembering the past but about **embodying the present**. When survivors learn to inhabit their bodies with safety and freedom, they lay the foundation for lasting recovery.

With this final therapeutic chapter, we now turn to the **conclusion of the book**, where we integrate the lessons from history, neuroscience, development, and healing practices charting a vision for trauma-informed futures.

CONCLUSION: TOWARD A TRAUMA-INFORMED FUTURE

Introduction

The study of trauma has transformed the fields of psychiatry, psychology, neuroscience, and public health. What was once dismissed as weakness or moral failure is now understood as a complex, biologically grounded, and socially mediated condition. Over the course of this book, we have traced trauma's rediscovery through the stories of Vietnam veterans, survivors of abuse, and countless others who refused silence. We have examined how trauma rewires the brain and body, shapes child development, fractures memory, and leaves survivors struggling with flashbacks, shame, and isolation. We have also explored paths to recovery from psychotherapy to neurofeedback, from community support to somatic therapies.

Now, in conclusion, we must ask: what does all this mean for the future? How can the insights of trauma studies be mobilized not only to heal individuals but also to transform systems, cultures, and societies?

This chapter will synthesize key themes and argue that the recognition of trauma presents both a challenge and an opportunity. If taken seriously, trauma science compels us to reimagine healthcare, education, justice, and community life. It demands that we address not only individual suffering but also the conditions that perpetuate violence and neglect. And it offers hope: by building trauma-informed societies, we can prevent cycles of harm and foster resilience across generations.

Trauma Is Both Universal and Individual

Trauma is not confined to war veterans or survivors of extreme abuse. It encompasses a broad spectrum of experiences from combat and disaster to domestic violence, childhood neglect, systemic racism, and poverty. Each individual's experience is unique, yet common biological and psychological patterns unite them.

Trauma Reshapes the Brain and Body

Neuroscience has shown that trauma is not "all in the head." It alters the stress response system, rewires fear circuits, and leaves lasting imprints on memory and perception. Survivors may live in chronic states of hypervigilance or dissociation, often without conscious awareness of why.

Childhood Trauma Is Foundational

Research on Adverse Childhood Experiences (ACEs) demonstrates that early trauma profoundly affects health, development, and lifespan. Neglect, abuse, and disrupted attachment increase the risk of mental illness, addiction, heart disease, and even premature death. Trauma in childhood is not only a personal tragedy but a major public health issue.

Recovery Is Possible—but Complex

Healing requires more than willpower. Effective recovery integrates multiple dimensions:

- **Psychological**: therapy, narrative processing, self-understanding.
- **Biological**: regulating the nervous system, restoring brain–body balance.
- **Social**: reconnecting with safe, supportive relationships.
- **Creative/embodied**: reclaiming agency through movement, art, and expression.

No single method heals trauma for all people; rather, recovery is a mosaic of strategies, tailored to the individual.

Trauma as a Public Health Crisis

The evidence is overwhelming: trauma is a root cause of numerous societal challenges, from chronic illness to addiction to cycles of violence. Addressing trauma is not only a mental health issue but a matter of social policy, economic productivity, and national well-being.

The Intergenerational Transmission of Trauma

Trauma is not confined to one lifetime. Epigenetic research suggests that severe stress can alter gene expression across generations. Children of survivors—whether Holocaust survivors, refugees, or victims of systemic oppression—often carry physiological and psychological echoes of trauma they did not personally endure.

Trauma and Social Justice

Recognizing trauma compels us to examine systemic forms of harm: racism, poverty, gender-based violence, mass incarceration. These are not just political issues; they are sources of ongoing traumatic stress. A trauma-informed society must confront the social structures that perpetuate suffering.

To create trauma-informed systems, several guiding principles emerge:

1. **Safety**: Physical and emotional safety must be foundational in healthcare, schools, workplaces, and communities.
2. **Trust and Transparency**: Institutions must be reliable and consistent, avoiding retraumatization through unpredictability or coercion.
3. **Empowerment**: Survivors should be supported in reclaiming choice and agency.
4. **Collaboration**: Healing is co-created, not imposed.
5. **Cultural Sensitivity**: Interventions must honor diverse traditions and ways of healing.

Healthcare

Doctors and nurses should be trained to recognize trauma symptoms, avoid invasive questioning, and practice patient-centered care. Trauma-informed healthcare improves treatment adherence and patient trust.

Education

Schools can either retraumatize students (through harsh discipline, punitive policies) or become spaces of healing (through predictable routines, supportive relationships, and social-emotional learning). Trauma-informed education reduces dropout rates and enhances academic success.

Justice System

Traditional justice often punishes trauma survivors rather than addressing root causes. Trauma-informed justice prioritizes rehabilitation, restorative practices, and alternatives to incarceration.

Community and Policy

Public policy can address trauma by investing in early childhood support, community mental health, and violence prevention. Building trauma-informed communities means prioritizing belonging, equity, and resilience.

Looking Forward with Hope

While trauma casts long shadows, recovery demonstrates the extraordinary resilience of the human spirit. Survivors who once lived in silence now lead advocacy movements. Communities ravaged by violence rebuild through reconciliation. Neuroscience continues to uncover pathways for brain and body healing.

The future of trauma studies lies not only in laboratories and clinics but also in **policy, education, and culture.** If societies embrace trauma-informed principles, the next generation may inherit a world better equipped to prevent suffering and foster resilience.

Responsibility and Renewal

Trauma is not an aberration it is part of the human story. But so too is healing. We now possess the knowledge to recognize trauma's imprints, to respond with compassion, and to prevent cycles of harm. The task is enormous, but the stakes are higher still: the well-being of individuals, families, and societies.

The call to action is clear: to move from a culture of silence and blame to one of acknowledgment and healing. To build systems that recognize trauma not as weakness but as an injury that can be treated. And to affirm, above all, that recovery is possible not only for individuals but for communities and nations.

By weaving together science, compassion, and collective responsibility, we can chart a path toward a trauma-informed future one where survival is not the end of the story, but the beginning of renewal.

www.ingramcontent.com/pod-product-compliance
Lightning Source LLC
LaVergne TN
LVHW022107200926
848481LV00003B/1078